Herbert Cushing Tolman

A Guide to the old Persian Inscriptions

Herbert Cushing Tolman

A Guide to the old Persian Inscriptions

ISBN/EAN: 9783743316690

Manufactured in Europe, USA, Canada, Australia, Japa

Cover: Foto ©ninafisch / pixelio.de

Manufactured and distributed by brebook publishing software (www.brebook.com)

Herbert Cushing Tolman

A Guide to the old Persian Inscriptions

THE BEHISTAN MOUNTAIN.

A GUIDE

TO THE

OLD PERSIAN

INSCRIPTIONS·

BY

HERBERT CUSHING TOLMAN, Ph. D. (YALE)

FOREIGN MEMBER OF THE ROYAL ASIATIC SOCIETY OF GREAT BRITAIN
AND IRELAND; ASSISTANT PROFESSOR OF SANSKRIT IN THE
UNIVERSITY OF WISCONSIN

NEW YORK ∴ CINCINNATI ∴ CHICAGO ∴ BOSTON ∴ ATLANTA
AMERICAN BOOK COMPANY

TO

MY HONORED TEACHER,

WILLIAM DWIGHT WHITNEY, Ph. D., LL. D.

*under whose instruction and guidance were spent five
years of my study in the Sanskrit language,*

this volume is

RESPECTFULLY DEDICATED.

TO THE READER.

This book does not claim to be a contribution to Iranian subjects. In these recent years there has been such an advancement in this line of scholarship that Sanskrit students have been compelled to surrender this field to specialists among whom in America the name of Dr. A. V. Williams Jackson of Columbia College is conspicuous. In 1862 Haug published an outline of Avesta grammar in the first edition of his essays. At that time seventy octavo pages were sufficient to contain the discovered material. Two years later Justi's grammar of one hundred and fifteen octavo pages was looked upon as practically exhaustive. The grammar of Spiegel appeared in 1867, that of de Harlez in 1878, that of Geiger in 1879. Kavasji Edalji's grammar (1891) and Jackson's grammar (1892) extend four fold the horizon of Avestan scholarship as contrasted with the outline presented by Haug thirty years before, although the same quantity of text of the Avesta is the basis for grammatical work. This statement can enable the reader to realize the great strides this study has made during a few years. My work in the Zend Avesta and in the dialects of Persia has been simply an avocation from my chosen field of Sanskrit.

No book has been published in English containing the grammar, text and vocabulary of all the Old Persian Inscriptions. It was this fact that induced the author in 1891 to issue a little volume entitled "Old Persian Grammar" the copies of which have now been sold. The first fifty pages of the present volume, which contain the grammatical principles, are based on this work.

The following features characterize this volume on Old Persian Inscriptions.

(1.) The grammatical principles arranged as a grammar of the language.

(2.) The complete classification of all the verb-forms occurring in the inscriptions.

(3.) The transliterated text. The portion supplied by conjecture has been inserted without brackets unless the conjectural reading be doubtful.

(4.) The references at the bottom of the page in the text which call the attention of the student to the grammar on the first occurrence of a form or principle.

(5.) The cuneiform text.

(6.) The translation.

(7.) The vocabulary giving the related words in Sanskrit, Latin, Gothic, Anglo-Saxon, etc.

The author recommends to the reader the following books as being of interest in the history of the early decipherment of the inscriptions:

(1.) Die altpersischen Keilinschriften nach Hrn. Westergaards Mittheilungen. Zeitschrift für die Kunde des Morgenlandes herausgegeben von Dr. Christian Lassen. Leipzig, 1845.

(2.) Die persischen Keilinschriften mit Uebersetzung und Glossar von Theodor Benfrey. Leipzig, 1847.

(3.) The Journal of the Royal Asiatic Society of Great Britain and Ireland, Vol. X, by H. C. Rawlinson. London, 1847.

(4.) Mémoire sur les inscriptions des Achéménides, conçues dans l' idiome des anciens Persans, par M. Oppert. Journal Asiatique ou recueil de mémoires d' extraits et de notices relatifs à l' histoire, à la philosophie, aux langues et à la litterature des peuples orientaux. Paris, 1851, 1852.

(5.) Expédition scientifique en Mésopotamie exécutée par ordre du Gouvernement de 1851 à 1854 par MM. Fulgence Fresnel, Félix Thomas et Jules Oppert, T. II. pp. 154–256.

(6.) Memoir on the Scythic Version of the Behistan Inscription by Edwin Norris, M. R. A. S. (Journal of the Royal Asiatic Society, Vol. XV, 1855.)

(7.) Mémoire sur les rapports de l' Égypte et de l' Assyrie dans l' antiquité éclaircis par l' étude des textes cunéiformes, par M. Jules Oppert. Paris, 1869.

(8.) Die altpersischen Keilinschriften im Grundtexte mit Uebersetzung. Fr. Spiegel, Leipzig, (two editions).

(9.) Zur Erklärung der altpersischen Keilinschriften von Dr. H. Kern. Zeitschrift der Deutschen morgenländischen Gesellschaft, Band XXIII, 1869.

(10.) Inscriptiones Palæo-Persicae. Cajetan Kossowicz, St. Petersburg, 1872.

In my references to foreign journals, I have used abbreviations as little as possible. They are mostly of the nature of the following and need not be explained.

ZDMG.=Zeitschrift der Deutschen morgenländischen Gesellshaft; f. vergl. Sprachforsch.=für vergleichende Sprachforschung; idg.=indogermanische; ai.=altindische; Wb.=Wörterbuch, etc., etc.

The author is aware of the many faults this book contains as fully as the severest critic can be, and he shall be glad to receive all suggestions which may make it more useful to the reader.

HERBERT CUSHING TOLMAN.

Madison, Wisconsin, November 4th, 1892.

TABLE OF CONTENTS.

GRAMMAR,	5
VERB-FORMS,	48
INSCRIPTIONS,	53
CUNEIFORM TEXT,	93
TRANSLATION,	115
VOCABULARY,	161

ABBREVIATIONS.

AOR., - - - Aorist	INF., - - - Infinitive
A. S., - Anglo Saxon	LAT., - - - Latin
AVEST, - - Avestan	PART., - Participle
CF., - - Compare	PERF. - - Perfect
ENG., - - English	PRES., - - Present
GERM., - - German	SKT., - - Sanskrit
GOTH., - - Gothic	SLAV., - - Slavonic
IMPF., - Imperfect	1. S., etc., 1st person singular, etc.
IMPV., - - Imperative	1. P., etc., 1st person plural, etc.

GRAMMAR.

PREFACE.

The Old Persian language deserves a larger place in American scholarship than it has yet received. Heretofore the work has been left entirely to European scholars, and it is due to a desire to awaken an interest in this old tongue among scholars of our own country that this little book has come into existence. I take the opportunity of expressing my gratitude to my pupil, WOLCOTT WEBSTER ELLSWORTH, a graduate of Yale and a member of the American Oriental Society, for help furnished me. He has taken my manuscript, which was in most part in the form of lectures, and arranged the whole work for the press. He also rendered much service in the transliteration of the cuneiform text.

I shall gladly receive all suggestions or corrections which may make this volume more helpful in imparting enthusiasm in the study of this our sister tongue.

H. C. T.

New Haven, Conn., June, 1891.

PREFACE TO SECOND EDITION.

The copies of the first edition are exhausted. The author has taken this opportunity to revise and amplify the whole work. He wishes to express his gratification for the kind reception the previous edition has received and also to make acknowledgment of many valuable suggestions. H. C. T.

Madison, Wis., Aug., 1892.

INTRODUCTION.

Professor Grotefend was the pioneer in the decipherment of the cuneiform text. His first discovery was announced in the Literary Gazette of Göttingen, in the year 1802. About one-third of the Old Persian alphabet was determined by his transliteration of the names of Cyrus, Darius, Xerxes and Hystaspes. Professor Rask added to this number the two characters representing M and N. A memoir of M. Burnouf published in June, 1836, and a work of Professor Lassen published at Bonn in May, 1836, entitled Die Alt-Persischen Keil-Inschriften von Persepolis, furnished a true determination of twelve additional characters. Dr. Beer, of Leipzig, in a review published in Allgemein. Hall. Literat. Zeitung in the year 1838, announced the discovery of the two characters for H and Y. M. Jacquet is said to have made the same discoveries independently at Paris, and also identified the equivalents for C and JH.

It is evident that a cursive style of writing was employed for epistolary purposes and had an existence contemporaneous with the cuneiform, since the character of the latter rendered it fit only for lapidary uses, [Cf. Daniel VI, 9; Nehemiah II, 9; Herodotus VII, 100.]. No Persian cuneiform writing appears after the time of Artaxerxes Ochus, and we are safe in saying that it died out at the end of the rule of the Achæmenian kings.

The oldest inscription is that of Cyrus the Great, which perhaps may be his sepulchral inscription although the epitaph quoted by Strabo and Ctesias differs from the one on this Old Persian monument. The latest is the inscription of Artaxerxes Ochus which exhibits many peculiarities of grammatical structure indicating the decay of the language. In this inscription two compound characters for BUM and DAH are introduced (cf. Cuneiform alphabet); also before this time in the tablets of Xerxes appears an ideogram for KHSHAY*A*THIY*A*, due undoubtedly to Semitic influences.

The most important of the inscriptions is the great inscription of Darius carved upon the sacred mountain Behistan [B*A*G*A* and ST*A*N*A* *place of God*]. This immense rock rose to a perpendicular height of 1700 feet from the plain below. On this conspicuous place Darius Hystaspes caused to be inscribed the history of his reign to be a legacy to succeeding generations. The figures of Darius and his attendants are executed with considerable skill, yet inferior to that shown in the bas-reliefs of Persepolis. Before Darius stand nine usurpers to the throne bound with a cord about their necks, while under the foot of the king lies the prostrate form of another. These are intentionally of rude design and small stature. Above the picture is the effigy of the Persian god Auramazda.

The Old Persian language is most closely related to the Vedic dialect of the Sanskrit, yet the interpretation of the inscriptions depends upon the combined aid of the Sanskrit and Avestan together with the surviving dialects of Persia which have been in any degree faithful to their mother tongue. Where the cognate or derivative word fails to appear in them, an arbitrary meaning must be assigned to the Old Persian to suit the context; hence I have given in the vocabulary the authority of the related languages for the signification of each word, wherever such authority can be obtained.

GRAMMAR.

PART I.
EUPHONY.

1. A conventional arrangement of the European letters, transliterating the Old Persian cuneiform characters, is as follows:

Vowels, simple { guttural, *a*, a.
palatal, i.
labial, u.

Diphthongs { palatal, *a*i, ai.
labial, *a*u, au.

	SURD.	SURD ASP.	SONANT.	NASAL.
Mutes { guttural,	k	kh	g	—
palatal,	c	—	j	—
dental,	t	th	d	n
labial,	p	f	b	m

Semivowels { palatal, y.
lingual, r.
labial, v.

Sibilants { lingual, sh.
dental, s.

Aspiration, h.

NOTE 1. The short a has no written sign (in the cuneiform text) unless it be initial. Therefore *a* (italic) has been used for this vowel in the transliteration. But when it is initial the same sign is employed for short a as for long a (vide infra), since the native characters make no distinction; e. g., ad*a*m

NOTE 2. The long a is transliterated in all cases by a simple a (in Roman type), e. g., Pars*a*.

EUPHONIC COMBINATION.

2. Two similar vowels coalesce, forming the corresponding long vowel; thus, p*a*sav*a* for p*a*sa and av*a*.

Actual examples can be cited of no vowels coalescing except a-vowels, yet undoubtedly should other successive vowels occur, they would suffer the above treatment.

3. The short *a* combines with a following i-vowel and u-vowel to *a*i and *a*u respectively; thus, Pars*a*iy for Pars*a* + iy; the long a to aī and aū; thus, aniyauva for aniya + uva.

NOTE. An example of a and I forming *a*i (as in the Sanskrit the long a and I combine into e [*a*i]) instead of aī, is found in the compound p*a*r*a*ita for p*a*ra and ita.

4. An i-vowel and u-vowel interpose their corresponding semivowel before a dissimilar vowel; thus, bumiya, bumi + a; isuvam, isu + am. Sometimes, however, the vowel is converted into its semivowel (especially if it be the final vowel of a diphthong); thus, ab*a*v*a*, for ab*a*u + a.

For exception, cf. dur*a*i*a*piy.

5. No vowel (except *a* and a) nor diphthong can end a word. There is inserted as a protection the corresponding semivowel; thus, up*a*riy, for up*a*ri; patuv, for patu; Pars*a*iy, for Pars*a*i.

NOTE 1. An exception seems to be adari (NRa).
NOTE 2. H*a*u retains the v even before ci, m*a*i, and t*a*i; e. g. h*a*uvci (I). Also occur p*a*ruvnam, p*a*ruvz*a*nanam.

6. Final a is sometimes made short before an enclitic; thus, av*a*d*a*shim, for av*a*dashim; m*a*n*a*ca, for m*a*naca. Many examples remain, however, of the long a preserved; thus, utam*a*iy, y*a*thasham, etc.

7. The semivowel is often connected with a preceding consonant by its corresponding vowel; thus, *a*durujiy*a*, for adurujy*a*.

8. A root is often expanded by vowel-insertion; thus, duruj, for druj (Skt. druh).

9. Every Old Persian word must end in **sh**, **m**, an a-vowel, or a semivowel. Should any other letters stand as finals etymologically, they are dropped; thus aja, for ajant.

10. The dental **s**, when preceded by any vowel except *a* and *a*, is changed into the lingual **sh**; thus, Darayavush, aisha, (for exceptions cf. isu, usatashana, Vaumisa, Nisaya): also after **kh**, and sometimes after **r**; thus, khshapa, adarshnaush, (but tarsatiy, Parsa, etc.).

NOTE. In the root had (originally sad) the influence of a preceding I is felt, even with the augment; thus, niyashadayam.

11. The final **s**, after being changed into **h**, is lost; thus, Parsa(h) martiya(h).

12. The dental before **t** is changed into **s** (as in Avestan); thus, basta, bound, for badta.

The semivowel **r** sometimes causes a preceding consonant to become aspirated; thus, cakhriya (from kar), Mithra, ufrastam.

14. Final **h** has gone over into the palatal **j** in the root duruj (Skt. druh), the influence of the aspiration being felt only in the form durukhtam. This exhibits the treatment of the palatal, namely, that it reverts to its original guttural if followed by any other sound than a vowel.

NOTE. Final h of thah becomes s before t; thus, thastanaiy.

15. Medial **h** has a tendency to fall away; thus, thatiy, for thahatiy; mahya for mahahya, (but Auramazdaha).

PART II.
ETYMOLOGY.
NOUNS AND ADJECTIVES.
CASE ENDINGS.

16. ENDINGS: Singular. A. The usual masculine and feminine ending in the nominative is **s**. Stems in *a* and **a** have allowed the **s** to pass over into **h** (cf. 11) which has dropped away, thus leaving the bare stem. Stems in **i** and **u** retain the **s** in the form **sh** (cf. 10). By consonant forms it is euphonically lost. Neuters(except *a*-stems, which add **m**) show the simple stem in this case. The pronominal ending for this gender is historically **t**, which is dropped at the end of a word, but changed to **sh** before the enclitic ciy. The common ending of the personal pronouns is *a*m (which is found also in the plural).

B. The accusative ends in **m** or *a*m in masculine and feminine nouns. The neuter has the same ending as the nominative.

C. The instrumental ending is **a**. In the pronominal declensions the nasal (**n**) is inserted between the stem and ending.

D. The ablative of *a*-stems doubtless ended in the historical **t** or **d**, which being final has been dropped euphonically (cf. 9). Elsewhere the ablative has the same ending as the genitive.

E. The genitive of *a*-stems adds hya (for original sy*a*). The ending of consonant stems is *a* for *a*h (original *a*s). Masculine stems in **i** and **u** have regularly the historic ending *a*s, the *a* of which combines with the vowel of the stem into ai (ai) and au, the s being preserved in the form sh (cf. 10). Feminine stems take the fuller ending, a for ah (original as) separated by an interspersed y.

F. The locative ending is i in consonant and *a*-stems, which appear euphonically in the form iy, aiy (cf. 5). In masculine u-stems this case ends in au (euphonically auv for an original avi). If this case occurred in a masculine i-stem, the form would be analogous, i. e., aiŋ(euphonically aiy for an original ayi). An artificial ending of feminine stems is the addition of a to the masculine ending; thus, auva, aiya. The true locative ending of this gender appears probably in one or two words in the form a, (duvaraya, dastaya? perhaps loc. dual, Arbiraya).

G. The vocative ends in the simple stem.

DUAL: A. The ending of the nominative, accusative, and vocative is a as in the Veda.

B. A doubtful form of the locative occurs as a, (dastaya.)

PLURAL: A. In the nominative the masculine and feminine ending aha appears, (corresponding to the Vedic asas). The shorter ending a, ah (original as) is also in use. Pronominal *a*-stems have the masculine nominative in ai. The neuter stems in *a* end in a.

B. The accusative ending is *a* for ah (original [*a*]ns) in consonant-stems. In *a*-stems the case appears in the form a. Neuter stems have this case like the nominative.

C. The instrumental has everywhere the form bish, uniting with *a*-stems into *a*ibish.

D. In the genitive the ending is am. In stems ending in a vowel, the nasal n is inserted, before which a short vowel is lengthened. In pronominal declensions s is the inserted consonant, before which *a* becomes *a*i.

E. The locative ending is suva. When preceded by *a* or a, the s passes over into h and is dropped, the form becoming uva. When preceded by other vowels the s is preserved, and the ending appears as shuva (cf. 10).

17. The normal scheme of endings is as follows:

	SINGULAR.	DUAL.	PLURAL.
N.	s(m)	a?	*a*h*a*, *a* (a)
A.	*a*m. m	a?	*a* (a)
I.	a	—	bish
Ab.	*a*	—	—
G.	*a*, (a)s, hya	a?	am
L.	i(a)	a?	suva, uva

For convenience in comparison the case endings in Sanskrit are added.

	SINGULAR.	DUAL.	PLURAL.
N.	s(m)	a(au)	*a*s*a*s, *a*s, (a)
A.	*a*m, m.	a(au)	*a*s, n, (a)
I.	a	bhyam	bhis, ais
D.	e	bhyam	bhy*a*s
Ab.	*a*s, (*a*d)	bhyam	bhy*a*s
G.	*a*s (as) s, sy*a*,	os	am
L.	i (am)au	os	su

DECLENSION I.

18. Stems (masculine and neuter) in *a*. Examples: b*a*g*a*, m., god; h*a*m*a*r*a*n*a*, n., battle.

SINGULAR.
N. b*a*g*a*
A. b*a*g*a*m
I. b*a*ga
Ab. b*a*ga
G. b*a*g*a*hya
L. b*a*g*a*iy
V. b*a*ga

SINGULAR.
N. h*a*m*a*r*a*n*a*m
A. h*a*m*a*r*a*n*a*m

DUAL.
N.A. b*a*ga? (g*a*usha)
L. b*a*g*a*ya? (d*a*st*a*ya)

PLURAL.
N. b*a*g*a*h*a*, b*a*g*a*
A. b*a*ga
I. b*a*g*a*ibish
G. b*a*g*a*nam
L. b*a*g*a*ishuva

PLURAL.
N. h*a*m*a*r*a*na
A. h*a*m*a*r*a*na

Examples of peculiar forms are:
A. The gen. sing. in hy*a* for hya (G*a*rm*a*p*a*d*a*hy*a*).
B. The abl. sing. in *a* for **a** (d*a*rsh*a*m*a*).
C. The loc. sing. in **y** for iy (dur*a*y).
D. The accusative of d*a*r*a*y*a* is identical with the stem in SZb.

DECLENSION II.

19. Stems (masculine) in **a**. Example: Aur*a*m*a*zda m., Auramazda.

SINGULAR.
N. Aur*a*m*a*zda
A. Aur*a*m*a*zdam
G. Aur*a*m*a*zdaha, or Aur*a*m*a*zdah*a*

DECLENSION III.

20. Stems (masculine) in **i** and **u**. Example of i-stem: Caishpi, m., Caishpis.

SINGULAR.
N. Caishpish
A. Caishpim
Ab. G. Caishpaish, or Caishpaish

Example of u-stem: gathu, m., place.

	SINGULAR.		PLURAL.
N.	gathush	G.	gathunam
A.	gathum		
I.	gathva		
Ab.G.	gathaush		
L.	gathauv		

NOTE: The genitive singular of Darayavau is Darayavahaush.

DECLENSION IV.

21. Stems (feminine) in **a**, **i**, and **u**. Example of a-stem: tauma, f., family.

	SINGULAR.		PLURAL.
N.	tauma	G.	taumanam
A.	taumam	L.	taumauva
Ab. G.	taumaya		
L.	taumaya or taumaya		

Example of i-stem: Bumi, f., earth.

SINGULAR.
N. bumish
A. bumim
Ab. G. bumiya

NOTE: The ending **sh** of the nominative singular is dropped before the enclitic shim in hiapism (Bh. I, 19).

Example of u-stem: d*a*hyu, f., country (perhaps irregular).

	SINGULAR.		PLURAL.
N.	d*a*hyaush	N.	d*a*hyav*a*
A.	d*a*hyaum or d*a*hyum	A.	d*a*hyav*a*
		G.	d*a*hyunam
L.	d*a*hy*a*uva	L.	d*a*hyushuva

DECLENSION V.

22. Stems in *a*r. Example: fr*a*mat*a*r m., leader.

SINGULAR.
N. fr*a*mata
A. fr*a*mat*a*r*a*m or fr*a*mat*a*r*a*m
G. fr*a*matr*a* (pitr*a*)

DECLENSION VI.

23. Stems ending in a consonant.
   A. Examples: n*a*pat, m., grandson; vith, m., clan.

SINGULAR.
N. n*a*pa
A. n*a*pat*a*m(?)
I. n*a*pata(?)
L. n*a*pati(?)

A. vith*a*m
I. vitha
L. vithi

PLURAL.
I. vithibish or vith*a*bis̠h

B. Stems in *a*n (m*a*n, v*a*n). Examples: Vi(n)-d*a*fr*a*n, m., Vindafra; nam*a*n, n., name; asman, m., heaven; khsh*a*tr*a*pav*a*n, m., satrap.

SINGULAR.
N. Vi(n)d*a*fra
A. Vi(n)d*a*fran*a*m

	SINGULAR.
N.	nama
A.	nama
A.	asmanam
N.	khshatrapava

C. Stems in *as*, *ish*. Examples: raucas, n., day; hadish, n., site.

	SINGULAR.		PLURAL.
N.	rauca	I.	raucabish
A.	rauca		
N.	hadish		
A.	hadish		

HETEROCLITES.

24. Nouns of other declensions have a tendency to assume forms of declension I. Thus, Khshayarshahya for Khshayarshaha; Darayava(h)ushahya for Darayavahaush; bumam for bumim; also nama sometimes takes the form of a feminine noun in **a**; thus, nama for nama.

COMPARISON OF ADJECTIVES.

25. The comparative and superlative endings are tara and tama; also iyas and ishta make corresponding forms of comparison.

PRONOUNS.

26. The pronouns of the first and second persons are thus declined: adam, I; tuvam, thou.

N.	adam	N.	vayam
A.	mam (enc. mam)	G.	amakham
Ab.	(enc. ma)		
G.	mana (enc. maiy)		

N. tuv*a*m
A. thuvam
G. (enc. t*a*iy, t*a*y, Bh. IV, 11.)

27. The demonstrative pronoun av*a* is declined as follows:

SING. M. F. N.
A. av*a*m — av*a* (with enc. ciy, av*a*shciy)
G. av*a*hya — av*a*hya

PLUR. M. F. N.
N. av*a*iy ava —
A. av*a*iy
G. av*a*isham — —

28. The declension of the other demonstrative h*a*uv (Skt. asau), that, he; ait*a* (Skt. et*a*t), this; and iy*a*m (Skt., ay*a*m), this, is as follows:

SING. M.
N. h*a*uv

SING. M. F. N. PLUR. M. F. N.
N. iy*a*m iy*a*m im*a* N. im*a*iy ima ima
A. im*a*m imam *A. im*a*iy ima ima
I. ana
G. — ahyaya, or ahiyaya

SING. M.
N. ait*a*
A. ait*a*

29. Enclitic forms of the pronoun of the third person are:

SINGULAR. PLURAL.
A. shim A. shish
G. sh*a*iy G. sham

A. dim A. dish

30. The declension of the relative (hy*a* [Skt. sy*a*] ty*a*m, etc.) is as follows:

	SING.	M.	F.	N.	PLUR.	M.	F.	N.
N.	hy*a*	hy*a*	ty*a*		N.	ty*a*iy	—	ty*a*
A.	ty*a*m		—		A.	ty*a*iy	—	—
I.	ty*a*na	—	—		G.	ty*a*isham	ty*a*isham	—

31. The interrogative pronoun occurs only in the vocative (masculine singular) ka. The indefinite pronoun is formed by adding the neuter of the pronominal stem ci; thus, k*a*sciy, cishciy.

32. The adjective aniy*a*, other, forms its neuter according to the pronominal declension; thus, aniy*a*shciy; its ablative is aniy*a*na, after the analogy of the instrumental. H*a*m*a*, all, has the genitive feminine singular h*a*m*a*hyaya.

VERBS.

33. The scheme of the normal endings of the verb is as follows:

PRIMARY ENDINGS.

	ACTIVE.		MIDDLE.	
	SING.	PLUR.	SING.	PLUR.
1.	mi	m*a*hy	*a*i	—
2.	hy	—	—	—
3.	ti	*a*(n)ti	t*a*i	—

SECONDARY ENDINGS.

1.	*a*m	ma	i	—
2.	(h)	—	—	—
3.	(t), s	*a*(n), sh*a*(n)	ta	*a*(n)ta

IMPERATIVE ENDINGS.

1.	—	—	—	—
2.	(*a*)di	ta	uva	—
3.	tu	—	tam	—

NOTE. The ending of the second person by appears in the form h*a* before the enclitic dish.

SUBJUNCTIVE MOOD.

34. The mood-sign of the subjunctive is *a*, which is added to the tense-stem. If the tense-stem end in *a*, the combination results in **a**. The inscriptions show the primary endings; thus, ah*a*tity from ah, b*a*vatiy from bu (tense-stem b*a*va).

OPTATIVE MOOD.

35. The inscriptions show ya as the mood-sign of the optative, which takes the regular series of secondary endings. Doubtless the simple **ī** was taken by the tense-stems in *a* and by the middle voice. The ya is connected with the stem by the union-vowel **ī**.

IMPERATIVE MOOD.

36. The imperative has no mood-sign; it adds its endings directly to the tense-stem.

AUGMENT.

37. The augment is a prefixed *a*. If the tense-stem begin with the vowel **ī** (or **u**) the augment combines with it into the strengthened diphthong **ai** (or **au**) instead of the regular *a*i, *a*u.

A. In a few cases the augment appears as **a**; thus, p*a*tiyab*a*ram. It is possible, however, to regard this **a** as the combination of the augment and the prefix **a**.

REDUPLICATION.

38. Old Persian reduplication shows the prefixion to a verb-root of its initial consonant and vowel.

A. A long vowel is made short in the reduplicating syllable; thus, ad*a*da from da.

B. A palatal is substituted for a guttural as the consonant of the reduplicating syllable; thus, c*a*khriya from k*a*r.

THE CONJUGATION-CLASSES.

39. The present system (composed of the indicative, subjunctive, optative and imperative) is divided into the following classes:

I. ROOT-CLASS.

In this class there is no class-sign; the personal endings are added directly to the root, unless there be a mood-sign, as in the subjunctive and optative.

II. REDUPLICATING-CLASS.

In this class the present-stem is formed by prefixing a reduplication to the root.

III. THE NU-CLASS.

This class forms its present-stem by adding the syllable nu, which is strengthened to *nau* in the singular.

IV. THE NA-CLASS.

The syllable na (in the plural ni) is added to the root to form the present-stem.

V. THE *A*-CLASS.

The present-stem is formed by adding *a* to the root, which (1) is strengthened or (2) remains unchanged.

VI. THE Y*A*-CLASS.

The class-sign is y*a*, which is added to the simple root.

VII. THE *A*Y*A*-CLASS.

This class adds *aya* to the strengthened root.

I. ROOT-CLASS.

40. Example: j*a*n, smite.

PRESENT INDICATIVE.

ACTIVE.		MIDDLE.	
SING.	PLUR.	SING.	PLUR.
1. j*a*(n)miy	j*a*(n)m*a*hy	j*a*n*a*iy	—
2. j*a*(n)hy	—	—	—
3. j*a*(n)tiy	j*a*n*a*(n)tiy	j*a*(n)t*a*iy	—

PRESENT SUBJUNCTIVE.

1. —	—	—	—
2. j*a*n*a*hy	—	—	—
3. j*a*n*a*tiy	?	j*a*n*a*t*a*iy	—

PRESENT OPTATIVE.

1. j*a*niyam	j*a*niyama	?	—
2. j*a*niya	—	—	—
3. j*a*niya	?	j*a*niyata	?

PRESENT IMPERATIVE.

1. —	—	—	—
2. j*a*(n)diy	j*a*(n)ta	j*a*nuva	—
3. j*a*(n)tuv	—	j*a*(n)tam	—

IMPERFECT.

1. aj*a*n*a*m	aj*a*(n)ma	aj*a*niy	—
2. aj*a*	—	—	—
3. aj*a*	aj*a*n*a*(n)	aj*a*(n)ta	aj*a*n*a*(n)ta

The form aitiy, (SZb) from root I shows that the root is strengthened, if it is able, in the three persons of the singular active.

As an example of a root beginning with I, illustrating the heavy augment, the form nijay*a*m (for nijai*a*m) from root I, 'go,' can be quoted.

The verb ah, be, preserves the original s before t. Its forms are as follows:

PRESENT INDICATIVE.

SINGULAR.	PLURAL.
1. amiy	am*a*hy
2. ahy	—
3. astiy	h*a*(n)tiy

PRESENT SUBJUNCTIVE.

3. . ah*a*tiy

IMPERFECT ACTIVE.

1. ah*a*m	—
2. —	—
3. ah*a*	ah*a*(n)

IMPERFECT MIDDLE.

3. ah*a*(n)ta and ah*a*(n)t*a*

II. REDUPLICATING-CLASS.

41. Example: da, put.
Present Imperative, 3. s., d*a*datuv.
Imperfect, 3. s., ad*a*da.

NOTE. The root sta, stand, takes the vowel i as reduplication, and shortens the stem-vowel; aisht*a*ta.

III. NU-CLASS.

42. Examples: j*a*d, ask; d*a*rsh, dare,
Present Imperative, 2. s., j*a*dn*a*utuv.
Imperfect, 3. s., ad*a*rshn*a*ush.

The verb k*a*r, do, shortens the root to ku in the present and imperfect. Its forms are as follows:

PRESENT SUBJUNCTIVE: SING. PLUR.
2. kun*a*vahy

IMPERFECT:
1. akun*a*v*a*m akuma (for akunu*ma)
3. akun*a*ush (in [S], akun*a*sh) akun*a*v*a*(n)

MIDDLE IMPERFECT:
3. akun*a*v*a*ta (in Bh. I, 12, akuta).

NOTE. The union-vowel *a* sometimes follows nu, which is strengthened to n*a*v; thus, varn*a*vatiy, kun*a*vahy, for varn*a*v*a*-*a*-ti, etc.

IV. NA-CLASS.

43. All forms of this class are regular (except Imperf. 1. s., adin*a*m, from di, for adinam); thus,

SINGULAR.
1. adin*a*m
2. adina, etc.

V. *A*-CLASS.

44. Examples: gub, call; bu, be; b*a*r, bear; jiv, live.

NOTE. In the following classes, the stem-final *a* is lengthened to a before m of the 1st personal endings, but is lost before *a*m of the 1st sing. imperf. and the 3d pl. endings, and the short *a* of the ending remains (or vice versa). The imperative takes no ending (unless it be *a*, which unites with the class-sign into a).

(1.) Examples of the strengthened root (corresponding to the unaccented *a*-class of the Sanskrit) are gub and bu. Roots in u (and i) strengthen their vowel to *a*u (and *a*i) which before the case-sign appears as *a*v (and *a*y).

PRESENT MIDDLE: SING. PLURAL.
3. g*a*ub*a*t*a*iy

PRESENT ACT. SUBJ.
2. b*a*vahy
3. b*a*vatiy

IMPERFECT.
1. ab*a*v*a*m
2. ab*a*v*a*
3. ab*a*v*a* ab*a*v*a*(n).

(2.) Examples of the unchanged root (corresponding to the accented *a*-class of the Sanskrit) are b*a*r and jiv.

PRESENT ACTIVE. SING.	PLURAL.
2. b*a*rahy	
3. b*a*ratiy	b*a*ra(n)tiy

PRESENT ACT. SUBJ.
2. b*a*rahy
3. b*a*ratiy

IMPERATIVE.
2. jiva
3. jiv*a*tuv

IMPERFECT ACTIVE.	
3. ab*a*ra	ab*a*ra(n)

IMPERFECT MIDDLE.	
3. ab*a*r*a*ta	ab*a*r*a*(n)ta

VI. Y*A*-CLASS.

45.

NOTE 1. The passive formation is the middle-endings added to the class-sign.

NOTE 2. The class-sign is often connected with the root by an interposed i.

Examples: duruj, deceive; m*a*r, die; th*a*h, say.

A. Examples of the simple class in active are duruj, m*a*r.

PRESENT ACTIVE, SING.
1. durujiyamiy

PRES. ACT. SUBJ.,
2. durujiyahy

IMPERFECT ACTIVE,
3. adurujiy*a*

IMPERFECT MIDDLE,
3. am*a*riy*a*ta

B. Example of the passive formation is th*a*h, which verb adds the active ending in the first person plural.

PRESENT, PLURAL.
1. th*a*hyam*a*hy

NOTE 3. The passive formation of k*a*r, do, is upon the strengthened stem; e. g., Imperf. 3. s., akun*a*vy*a*ta.

NOTE 4. It is possible to regard the form ath*a*hy*a* as the imperfect 3d sing., with the active ending, instead of the middle, yet possessed of a passive sense. I prefer to read, however, ath*a*hy, believing it to be the passive aorist with short vowel in the stem. (Cf. 50 N.)

VII. A YA-CLASS.

46.

NOTE 1. A causative conjugation is made from this class, but all verbs belonging to this class have not a causative value.

NOTE 2. The class-sign is added to the strengthened root.

Examples: d*a*r, hold; ish, send; sta, stand.

A. Examples of the simple class are d*a*r, and ish.

Present, 1. s., dar*a*yamiy

Imperfect, 3. s., adar*aya*

IMPERFECT, SING.
1. aish*aya*m
2. aish*aya*

B. Example of the causative conjugation is sta.

IMPERFECT, SING.
1. astay*a*m
3. astay*a*

NOTE 3. Sometimes the class-sign appears as ay*a*; thus, ag*a*rbay*a*m, ag*a*rbay*a*, etc.

Verbs sometimes make their formation in more than one class; thus, j*a*diyamiy and j*a*dn*a*utuv.

THE PERFECT.

47. The Old Persian has left us only one example of the perfect; i. e., Optative, 3 s., cakhriya from k*a*r.

THE AORIST.

48. There have been preserved two aorists; (1) the root aorist, which adds the personal endings directly to the root, and (2) the sibilant aorist, which takes sa as a tense-sign. An example of the root aorist is the form ada, 3d person singular of da. Examples of the sibilant aorist are aisha, 3d person sing., and aisha(n), 3d person plur. of root I.

49. The aorist adds the secondary endings to the tense-stem, to which the augment has been prefixed.

50. The root-aorist has a peculiar formation, which is passive in meaning, corresponding to what the Hindu grammarians call the "passive aorist" of the Sanskrit. The third person singular of the middle is the only form in use. This person is made by adding i (which it has borrowed from the first person) to the root. Euphonically, the form appears as iy or y. The root is usually strengthened; thus, adariy or adary from dar.

NOTE. In the root thah, the stem-vowel remains short; thus, athahy (for athahy). The Hindu grammarians mention certain roots of the Sanskrit in am, which preserve the short a; thus, agami, avadhi, etc.

51. The optative of the root-aorist doubtless appears in agamiya from gam.

NOTE. The root bu loses its stem-vowel in this mode; e. g., biya.

FUTURE.

52. The Old Persian has left no future-system. A periphrastic future is built out of a nomen agentis and the auxiliary bu; thus, jata biya (Bh. IV, 17), let him be a killer; i. e., let him kill (he shall kill).

PASSIVE PARTICIPLE.

53. The passive participle is formed by adding ta to the simple root; thus, karta from kar.

INFINITIVE.

54. The Old Persian infinitive is formed by the suffix tana (Lat. tinus in crastinus, diutinus) which appears always in the locative case; thus, ka(n)tanaiy from kan.

NOTE. The infinitive of kar changes the initial guttural of the root to a palatal: e. g., cartanaiy.

PREPOSITIONS.

55. With accusative: abiy, antar, athiy, upariy, upa, patiy, patish, pariy.
With instrumental: patiy, hada.
With genitive: abish, patiy, pasa.
With ablative: haca.
With locative; anuv, patiy.

VERBAL PRFFIXES.

56. atiy—across, beyond   ud, us—up, out.
    apa—away, forth.   upa—to, towards.
    ava—down, off.   ni—down, into.
    a—to, unto.   nij—out, forth.
        para—away, forth.
        fra—forward, forth.
        ham—together.

PRIMARY SUFFIXES.

57. a, a, ah, i, ish, u, tar (forming nouns of agency and relationship), ti, tu, tha, thi, thu, tra, da, na, man, ma, ya, yu, ra.

SECONDARY SUFFIXES.

58. iya, pertaining to (used also to form the patronymic).
aina, consisting of.
ka (an adjectival suffix).
ta (having an ablative value and often used for that case).
ta (adverbial suffix).
tha (having a local sense).
da (adverbial suffix).
na (adjectival suffix).
ra (adjectival suffix).
van, 'possessed of.'

PART III.
SYNTAX.

59. Although the Old Persian language can be called syntactical, yet there exist many traces of that loose and free construction (paratax) which is original to speech.

USES OF THE NUMBERS.

60. One or two peculiar constructions call for notice.

A. A collective noun in the singular often has the government of a plural noun, both over a verb and a pronoun; thus, imam bumim......tyasham adam athaham ava akunavata (NRa) 'This earth...... what I commanded them (i. e., this earth) this was done.'

B. The singular of the personal pronoun adam can be expanded in a following clause into the plural; thus, patish mam hamaranam cartanaiy pasava hamaranam akuma. (Bh. I, 19) 'to engage in battle against me, afterwards we engaged in battle.'

C. The plural can be used for the dual; thus, avathasham hamaranam kartam (Bh. II, 6) 'thus the battle was fought by them.' (i. e., the army of Vidarna and the rebellious army); Anamakahya mahya II raucabish (Bh. I, 19) 'on the 2d day of the month Anamaka' (lit., with two days).

USES OF THE CASES.
THE NOMINATIVE.

61. The nominative is the case of the subject of a finite verb, and of all words qualifying the subject, both attributively, predicatively, and appositionally. A few peculiar uses are to be noticed.

A. The nominative is used often in the weak syntax common to the Old Iranian languages. Artificially it can be explained as the subject of astiy supplied, the idea being repeated in the form of a pronoun; thus, martiya Frada nama avam mathishtam akunava(n)ta (Bh. III, 3) 'a man, Frada by name, him they made chief.'

NOTE 1. The pronoun is sometimes omitted, leaving the nominative where the accusative of the direct object would be expected; adam fraishayam Dadarsis nama Parsa mana ba(n)daka (Bh. III, 2) 'I sent forth my subject, Dadarsis by name, a Persian.'

NOTE 2. This free use of the nominative is shown in such expressions as Kuganaka nama vadanam (Bh. II, 3) 'there is a town, Kuganaka by name; (lit. there is a town, [its] name is Kuganaka). That nama is nominative, not accusative, is shown by the fact that it sometimes agrees in gender with the noun, if that be feminine, e. g., Sikatyauvatish nama dida Nishaya nama dahyaush (Bh. I, 13) 'there is a stronghold, Sikatyauvatis by name; there is a country, Nishaya by name.'

B. The nominative is used in the predicate after a verb in the middle voice which has the force of a passive; thus, hya Nabuk(u)dracara agaubata (Bh. I, 19) 'who called himself (i. e. was called) Nabukudracara.'

THE VOCATIVE.

62. The vocative is the case of direct address.

The following peculiarity needs to be considered, namely: The vocative of the personal pronoun tuvam is made indefinite by the insertion of the interrogative ka in the same case; thus, tuvam ka hya aparam imam dipim vainahy (Bh. IV, 15) 'O thou (whoever thou art) who wilt hereafter see this inscription.'

THE ACCUSATIVE.

63. The accusative is the case of the direct object of a verb, and of all words which qualify the object, both attributively, predicately, and appositionally; e. g. Auramazda hya imam bumim ada (O.) 'Auramazda who created this earth.'

64. Some verbs which allow two constructions may take two accusatives, one in each construction; e. g., verbs of asking, taking, etc.; as aita adam Auramazdam jadiyamiy (NRa.) 'I beg this of Auramazda.' khshatramshim adam adinam (Bh. I, 13). 'I took the kingdom from him.'

A. The verbs kar and da admit two accusatives, one as object, the other as predicate; thus, hya Darayava(h)um khshayathiyam akunaus. (O.) 'who made Darius king;' hauv Darayava(h)um khshayathiyam adada (H.), 'he has made Darius king.'

B. A few verbs strengthen the verbal notion by adding their past passive participle, which becomes an accusative in agreement with the direct object; thus, avam (h)ubartam abaram (Bh. I, 8) 'I supported him well; (lit, him well supported I supported.)'

65. The accusative can follow nouns which have such a verbal character that they share the construction of a verb; thus, Auramazda thuvam dausta biya (Bh. IV, 16) 'may Auramazda be a friend to you.'

66. The accusative stands as the limit of motion, both with and without a preposition; thus, yatha mam kama (Bh. IV, 4) 'as the wish (came) to me' (i. e. as my wish was); adam (karam) fraishayam Uvajam, (Bh. I, 17) 'I sent an army to Susiana;' Ka(m)bujiya Mudrayam ashiyava (Bh. I, 10) 'Cambyses went to Egypt;' (karam) fraishaya abiy Vivanam (Bh. III, 9) 'he sent the army to Vivana.'

67. The accusative expresses extent and duration, both with and without a preposition; thus, khshapava raucapativa ava akunavayata (Bh. I, 7) 'this was done day and night.'

A. The time in which an action took place seems to have been expressed at times by the accusative. One case occurs in the inscriptions; Garmapadahya mahya I rauca thakata aha avathasham hamaranam kartam (Bh. III, 1.) 'on the first day of the month Garmapada then it was that thus the battle was fought by them.' This idiom appears occasionally in Sanskrit.

68. The accusative of specification defines the application of a noun; thus, haca Pirava nama rauta (SZb.) 'from a river, the Nile by name.' Cf. 61, A. n. 2.

THE INSTRUMENTAL.

69. The instrumental is the case denoting association and accompaniment originally, and as a derived notion, instrument and means.

70. The instrumental of accompaniment usually takes the preposition hada; thus, aisha hada kara (Bh. I, 19) 'he went with his army.'

A. In enumeration the instrumental may be used in the sense of association, when the same case as the preceding nouns would be expected; thus abacaris gaithamca maniyamca v(i)thibishca .... avastayam (Bh. I, 14) 'I restored the commerce and the cattle and the dwellings and together with the clans' (i. e., and the clans.)

71. The instrumental of means or instrument is very frequent; thus, vashna Auramazdaha (Bh. I, 5.) 'by the grace of Auramazda.' ardastana .... vithiya karta (L.) 'the lofty structure was made by the clan.'

72. The prosecutive instrumental denotes the association of time with an event; thus, Viyakhnahya mahya XIV raucabish thakata aha yadiy udapatata

(Bh. I, 11) 'on the 14th day of the month Viyakhna, then it was when he rose up (lit. in connection with 14 days).' . Cf. 67, A.

73. The instrumental is sometimes used in the sense of the locative, denoting the point in space; thus, ad*a*mshim gathva avastay*a*m (Bh. I, 14) 'I put it in its place.' m*a*na data ap*a*riyay*a*(n) (Bh. I, 8) 'they followed in my law.' v*a*siy aniy*a*sciy n*a*ib*a*m kart*a*m ana Parsa (D.) 'there is many another beautiful work in this Persia.'

THE DATIVE.

74. The dative case has no existence in Old Persian, its place being taken by the genitive.

THE ABLATIVE.

75. The use of the ablative is to express separation or distinction. The preposition h*a*ca is usually joined to this case.

76. The ablative denotes issue, removal, release, and like relations; thus, khsh*a*tr*a*m ty*a* h*a*ca amakh*a*m t*a*umaya p*a*rab*a*rt*a*m ah*a* (Bh. I, 14) 'the kingdom which was taken from our family.' h*a*uv h*a*cama h*a*mitriy*a* ab*a*v*a* (Bh. III, 5) 'he became estranged (rebellious) from me.'

A. The notion of this ablative passes over to that of cause; thus, kar*a*shim h*a*ca d*a*rsh*a*m*a* at*a*rs*a* (Bh. I, 13) 'the state feared him on account of (his) violence.'

77. The ablative expresses defense, which is a development of the idea of removal; thus, h*a*ca dr*a*uga patip*a*y*a*uva (Bh. IV, 5) 'protect yourself from deceit.' imam d*a*hyaum Aur*a*m*a*zda patuv h*a*ca h*a*inaya h*a*ca d(u)shiyara h*a*ca dr*a*uga (H.) 'may Auramazda protect this province from an army, from failure of crops, and from deceit.'

A. The ablative follows tars, to fear. Such an ablative contains this same idea of removal (i. e., recoil from a dread object). haca aniyana ma tarsam (I) 'let me not fear a foe.'

78. The ablative is the case of comparison. This use is simply a special application of its original notion of distinction; thus, apataram haca Parsa (NRa) 'another than a Persian' (lit. another from a Persian.)

THE GENITIVE.

79. The true use of the genitive is to qualify a noun with the same powers as the adjective enjoys. The genitive, however, did not remain restricted to this adjectival construction, but is employed with verbs and adjectives.

80. The subjective genitive, including the author and possessor, expresses the subject of the action; thus vashna Auramazdaha adam khshayathīya amiy (Bh. I, 5) 'by the grace of Auramazda, I am king.'

A. The genitive regularly follows kartam, perhaps on account of a substantive idea in the participle; thus, avathasham hamaranam kartam (Bh. III, 10) 'thus the battle was fought by them.'

NOTE. The genitive expressing means is found in Sanskrit.

B. The genitive follows pasa; thus, kara Parsa pasa mana ashiyava (Bh. III, 6) 'The Persian army followed me.'

C. The genitive expresses manner; thus, hamahyaya tharda (Bh. IV, 7) 'in every way.'

81. The partitive genitive denotes the whole of which a portion is taken; thus, adam Darayava(h)ush khshayathiya khshayathiyanam (Bh. I, 1) 'I am Darius, the king of kings.'

A. The genitive is dependent on an adjective (especially a superlative) which has substantival character enough to allow a partitive construction; thus Auramazda hya mathishta baganam (F.) 'Auramazda, who is the greatest of the gods.'

82. The objective genitive, which designates the noun as the object of the action, occurs nowhere in the inscriptions.

83. The datival genitive expresses the indirect object; thus, karahya avatha athaha (Bh. I, 16) 'thus he said to the state.' Auramazda khshatram mana frabara (Bh. I, 5) 'Auramazda gave the kingdom to me.'

NOTE. This use is simply a pregnant construction of the possessive genitive; e. g., khshatram mana frabara, he gave the kingdom to me (made it mine by giving). This same power of the genitive is shared by the Prakrit and the late Sanskrit.

A. The verb duruj, "to deceive,' is followed by the genitive once in the inscriptions; elsewhere it governs the accusative. Karahya avatha adurujiya Bh. I, 11 'thus he deceived the people.'

B. The genitive enclitic sham follows ajanam in place of the accusative of direct object in Bh. IV, 2 adamsham ajanam, 'I smote them,' and patiyakshaiy NRa.

THE LOCATIVE.

84. The locative is the case denoting location and condition. The locative expresses situation, both with and without a preposition; thus, adam khshayathiya Parsaiy (Bh. I, 1) 'I am king in Persia.' hya Madaishuva mathishta aha Bh. II, 6 'who was greatest among the Medes.' vardanam anuv Ufratauva (Bh. I,(19) 'a town on the Euphrates.'

A. The locative takes the place of the instrumental in the expression nipadiy, 'on foot;' e.g., atiyaisha.

p*a*sav*a* Vivan*a* h*a*da kara nip*a*diy (Bh. III, 11) 'afterwards Vivana followed with his army on foot.'

B. The locative can take the place of the partitive genitive; thus, Mad*a*ishuv*a* m*a*thishta (Bh. II, 6) 'the greatest among the Medes.'

THE PECULIARITIES OF THE INSCRIPTIONS OF ARTAXERXES MNEMON AND ARTAXERXES OCHUS.

85. These inscriptions exhibit such careless irregularities that they call for special treatment.

A. The nominative is attracted into the case of the preceding noun, although the predicate appears in the nominative; thus, thatiy Art*a*khsh*a*tra Dar*a*yav*a*(h)ush*a*hya khshay*a*thiy*a*hya putr*a* Dar*a*y*a*v*a*(h)ush*a*hya Artakhsh*a*thrahya khshay*a*thiy*a*hy*a* putr*a* (S.) 'says Artaxerxes, the son of Darius, the king; Darius (was) the son of Artaxerxes, the king.'

B. The nominative appears for the accusative with a qualifying pronoun in the accusative; im*a*m ap*a*dan*a* (S.) '(Darius made) this structure.'

C. The genitive is attracted into the case of the subject or the predicate nominative and appears in the nominative; thus, Art*a*khsh*a*tra Dar*a*yav*a*(h)ush khshay*a*thiy*a* putr*a* (P.) 'Artaxerxes, son of Darius, the king.'

D. The nominative is thrust into the accusative, yet the passive construction is retained; thus, im*a*m usat*a*sh*a*nam atha(n)g*a*nam mam upa mam k*a*rta (P.) 'this stone lofty structure was built by me for myself.'

E. The accusative expresses means, taking the place of the regular genitive construction after k*a*rt*a*m; thus, ty*a* mam k*a*rta (P.) 'what was done by me.'

F. A substantive in the singular takes its participle in the plural; thus, ty*a* mam k*a*rta (P.) 'what was done by me.'

THE ADJECTIVE.

86. The adjective and the participle agree with the substantive in gender, number, and case.
A few peculiar cases are to be noticed.

A. The adjective can be hardened into a neuter substantive and in this way enter into the relation of an appositive or a predicate noun; thus, ciykaram ava dahyava (NRa.) 'beautiful are the regions (lit. a beauty these regions are). hauv kamanam aha (Bh. II, 6) 'that was faithful (lit. a faithful thing).'

B. The adjective is used, most often in the singular, to take the place of the name of a country; thus, Parsa, 'Persia (lit. Persian).' Mada, Media (lit. Median).'

NOTE 1. Sometimes the plural occurs, and in a few cases alternates with the singular; thus, Yauna and Yauna (NRa) 'Ionia (lit. Ionian and Ionians).'

NOTE 2. The real name of the country appears a few times; thus, Uvarazmish (NRa.), Harauvatish (Bh. I, 6).

C. The noun vith, 'clan,' when used appositionally takes the place of the regular adjective vithiya; thus, hada v(i)thibish bagaibish (H.) 'with (his) fellow gods (lit. with the gods [namely his] fellows).'

D. In the inscriptions of Artaxerxes Ochus the masculine of the pronoun agrees with the feminine noun; thus, imam usatashanam (P.) 'this lofty structure.'

PRONOUNS.

87. The demonstrative pronouns ava and hauv supply the place of the third personal pronoun.

88. The relative pronoun tya, beside enjoying its ordinary functions, has the following important uses:

A. The relative pronoun frequently serves to connect the noun with whatever qualifies it, either appositionally, adjectively, adverbially, genitively, or locatively. In this capacity its independent character is lost and it agrees with its antecedent, not only in gender and number but also in case, thus becoming the equivalent of the Greek article; thus, v(i)th*a*m tyam amakh*a*m (Bh. I. 14) 'the clan of ours.' ty*a*na m*a*na data (Bh. I, 8) 'in my law.' khsh*a*tr*a*m ty*a* Babir*a*uv (Bh. I, 16) 'the kingdom at Babylon.' kar*a*m ty*a*m Mad*a*m (Bh. II, 6) 'the Median army.' Nabuk(u)dr*a*c*a*r*a* amiy hy*a* Nabunit*a*hya putr*a* (Bh. II, 16) 'I am Nabukudracara the son of Nabunita.'

B. The relative can be used in the place of a demonstrative; thus, kar*a*m fræish*a*y*a*m ty*a*ip*a*tiy (Bh. II, 13) 'I sent an army against these.'

USES OF THE VOICES.

89. There are (as in Sanskrit) two voices, active and middle. The passive notion is conveyed through the middle voice by means of a definite class-sign.

One or two peculiar constructions call for notice.

A. The active with direct object can take the place of the middle; thus, thuvam maty*a* durujiyahy (Bh. IV, 6) 'do not deceive yourself.'

B. The middle without the passive sign sometimes contains the passive signification; thus, hy*a* N*a*buk(u)-dr*a*c*a*r*a* ag*a*ub*a*ta (Bh. I 19) 'who was called (lit. called himself) N*a*bukudracara.' ag*a*rbay*a*ta (Bh. II, 13) 'he was taken.' an*a*yata (Bh. I, 17) 'he was led.'

C. The passive participle of neuter verbs has no passive notion, but simply an indefinite past tense; thus h*a*(n)gm*a*ta (Bh. II, 7) 'having come together.'

USES OF THE MOODS.

THE INDICATIVE.

90. The indicative is used in the recital of facts.

THE SUBJUNCTIVE.

91. The subjunctive has a general future meaning, denoting what is possible and probable. This use is perhaps the historic one from which the nicer and more elaborate values of this mood in the cognate languages have been developed; thus, tuvam ka hya aparam imam dipim patiparsahy (Bh. IV, 6) 'O thou who wilt hereafter examine this inscription.'

A. Conditional sentences introduced by yadiy, 'if', take their verbs in the subjunctive; thus yadiy avatha maniyahy (Bh. IV, 5) 'if thus thou thinkest.'

B. Purpose clauses introduced by yatha, 'in order that', take their verbs in the subjunctive; thus, yatha khshnasahy (NRa.) 'in order that you may know.'

C. The negative matya (ma and tya) denoting purpose or warning takes the subjunctive; thus, matya mam khshnasatiy (Bh. I, 13) 'that (the state) may not know me.'

D. The subjunctive with the negative matya is used to express prohibition, less peremptory than the imperative, more so than the optative; thus, patikara matya visanahy (Bh. IV, 15) 'thou shalt not destroy (these) pictures.'

E. The temporal conjunction yava takes the subjunctive in its ordinary future sense; thus, yava tauma ahatiy (Bh. IV, 16) 'as long as (thy) family shall be.'

THE OPTATIVE.

92. The optative denotes what is desired, in which capacity it is the equivalent of a mild imperative. In a weakened sense it denotes what may or can be.

A. The optative with the negative particle ma expresses a desired negation, not direct prohibition; thus, utataiy tauma ma biya (Bh. IV, 11) 'may there not be a family of thine.'

THE IMPERATIVE.

93. The imperative expresses a command or a desire; thus, paraidiy avam jadiy (Bh. II, 7) 'go, smite that (army).'

THE INFINITIVE.

94. The infinitive, in its fundamental and usual sense, expresses purpose, as the dative infinitive of the Veda. It has also become employed in a freer sense as the simple complement of a verb; thus, aisa hada kara patish mam hamaranam cartanaiy (Bh. I, 19) 'he went with (his) army against me to engage in battle,' kasciy naiy adarshnaush cisciy thastanaiy pariy Gaumatam (Bh. I, 13) 'no one dared to say anything against Gaumata.'

USES OF THE TENSES.

95. A few peculiar uses deserve notice.

A. The present with duvitataranam denotes that the action was begun in the past and continues in the present. This peculiarity is to be compared with the Latin use of the present with iam diu, etc.

B. The indicative forms of the imperfect and aorist appear without augment. With the loss of this augment the imperfect and aorist sacrifice their own peculiar character and take on other notions. After ma prohibitive the sense is that of a subjunctive or optative; thus, haca aniyana ma tarsam (I.) 'may I not fear an enemy.'

C. Yata in the sense of "while" takes the imperfect; in the sense of "until" it takes either the imperfect or aorist.

D. The passive participle, both with and without an auxiliary verb, is used in the sense of a passive perfect; thus, amata am*a*hy (Bh. I, 3) 'we have been tested (or prolonged).' B*a*rdiy*a* av*a*jat*a* (Bh. I, 10) 'Bardiya was slain.'

DEPENDENT CLAUSES.

96. Final Clauses. Cf. 91, B. and C.

97. Consecutive Clauses. Ty*a* (the neuter of the relative) introduces clauses expressing result, and takes the verb in the indicative; thus, dr*a*ug*a*dish h*a*mitriya akun*a*ush ty*a* im*a*iy kar*a*m adurujiy*a*sha(n) (Bh. IV, 4) 'a lie made them rebellious so that they deceived the people.'

98. Conditional Clauses. Cf. 91, A.

99. Causal Clauses. Y*a*tha expressing cause takes the verb in the indicative; thus, Aur*a*mazda up*a*stam ab*a*ra......yatha n*a*iy arik*a* ah*a*m'(Bh. IV, 13) 'Auramazda gave aid, because I was not unfriendly.'

100. Temporal Clauses.

A. Y*a*tha, "while," takes the indicative; "in order that," the subjunctive.

B. Yata, Cf. 95, C.

C. Yava, "as long as," prefers the subjunctive. Cf. 91, E.

INDIRECT DISCOURSE.

101. A form of indirect narrative is hardly developed in the language. Statements are expressed

usually in the most simple direct manner; thus, yadiy avatha maniyahy dahyaushmaiy duruva ahatiy (Bh. IV, 5) 'if thus thou thinkest, may my country be safe.'

A. This influence of the direct form of statement is felt often by the pronoun in a dependent clause; thus, karam avajaniya matyaman khshnasatiy (Bh. I, 13) 'he would smite the people that they may not know him (lit. that they may not know me)'; the idea being expressed as it was conceived in the mind of the author.

B. A tendency towards indirect discourse is manifested by the use of the neuter of the relative tya; thus, karahya naiy azda abava tya Bardiya avajata (Bh. I, 10) 'there was ignorance on the part of the state that Bardiya was slain.'

NOTE. The relative pronoun yat in Sanskrit appears to have a few times this same function. I refer to a case I have met recently in my reading, namely in the Khandogya Upanishad.

COMPOUNDS.

102. Copulative. The composition of two nouns in coordinate construction as if connected by the conjunction "and" does not appear in the inscriptions.

103. Determinative. The composition of two words, the former of which qualifies the second, either as a noun in case relation, adjective, or verb, occurs; thus, sarastibara, 'having bows', Auramazda, asabara, etc.

104. Adjective. The determinative compound by assuming the idea of "possessing" becomes an adjective; thus, Artakhshatra, 'Artaxerxes' (as a determi-

native, 'lofty kingdom'; as an adjective compound, "possessing a lofty kingdom'.) zur*a*k*a*ra, 'possessing power as action', (h)uv*a*sp*a*, p*a*ruz*a*n*a*, etc.

NOTE. The compound p*a*ruz*a*na has its two members separated, yet preserves the meaning and value of a compound; thus, p*o*ruv z*a*nanan (Ca) (Cb) (K).

102. Prepositional. The composition of two words, the former of which is a preposition governing the second, is found often; thus, p*a*sav*a*, 'after this', tar*a*d*a*ray*a* p*a*tip*a*d*a*m fr*a*h*a*rv*a*m, etc.

VERB-FORMS.

A complete classification of all the verb-forms ocring in the Old Persian language,

Aj (?), drive.   (See vocabulary.)
Impf. 3. s., aj*a*ta.

Akhsh (?), see.   (See vocabulary.)
Impf. 1. s., akhsh*a*iy.

Ah. be.

Pres. 1. s., amiy; 2. s., ahy, 3. s., astiy; 1. p.; am*a*hy: 3. p., h*a*(n)tiy; 3. s., ah*a*tiy(subj.).   Impf. 1. s., ah*a*m; 3. s., ah*a*; 3. p., ah*a*(n); 3. p. (middle) ah*a*(n)ta, (ah*a*[n]t*a*).

Av*a*h, ask aid.

Impf. (middle) 1. s., av*a*h*a*iy.

I, go.

Pres. 3. s., aitiy; 2. s., idiy (impv.); 2. p.; ita (impv.) Impf. 1. s., ay*a*m, 3 p., ay*a*(n).   Aor. 3. s., aish*a*; 3. p., aish*a*(n). Part., it*a*

Ish, send.

Impf. 1. s, aish*a*y*a*m 3. s., aish*a*y*a*.

K*a*n, dig.

Pres. 3. s., k*a*(n)tuv (impv.).   Impf. 1. s., ak*a*n*a*m; 3. s., ak*a*.   Aor. (passive) 3. s., ak*a*niy.   Inf. k*a*(n)t*a*n*a*iy.

.K*a*r, do.

Pres. 2. s., kun*a*vahy (subj.), k*a*rahy (subj.) 2. s. k*a*ra (impv.) Impf. 1. s., akun*a*v*a*m; 3. s., akun*a*ush, (akun*a*sh: S), 1. p., akum*a*, 3. p. akun*a*v*a*(n), 3. s. (middle) akun*a*v*a*ta, 3. p. akun*a*v*a*(n)ta, (akuta), 3. s. (passive) akun*a*vy*a*ta; Perf. 3. s. c*a*khriy*a* (opt.). Inf. c*a*rt*a*n*a*iy; Part k*a*rt*a*.

Khshi (?), rule. (See vocabulary.)
Impf. (middle) 1. s, akhsh*a*iy.

Khshnas, know.
Pres. 2. s. khshnasahy (subj.), 3. s. khshnasatiy (subj.)

G*a*m, go.
Aor. 3. s. gm*a*ta, 3. s. j*a*miya (opt). Part gm*a*ta.

G*a*rb, seize.
Impf. 1. s. ag*a*ray*a*m, 3. s., ag*a*rbay*a*, 3. p. ag*a*rbay*a*(n), 3. s. (middle) ag*a*bay*a*ta,

Gud, hide.
Pres. 2. s. g*a*ud*a*yahy (subj.); Impf. 3, s. ag*a*ud*a*ya.

Gub, speak.
Pres. (middle) 3. s. g*a*ub*a*t*a*iy, 3. s. g*a*ubat*a*iy (subj.); Impf. 3. s. ag*a*ub*a*ta.

J*a*d, ask.
Pres. 1. s. j*a*diyamiy, 3. s. j*a*d*a*n*a*utuv (impv.)

J*a*n, smite.
Pres, 2. s. j*a*diy (impv.), 2. p. jata (impv.) j*a*niya (opt.); Impf. 1 s. aj*a*nam, 3. s. aj*a*, 3 p. aj*a*na (n); Part. j*a*ta.

Jiv, live.
Pres. 2. s. jiv*a*hy, 2. s. jiva (impv.)

T*a*khsh, fashion.
Impf. (middle) 1 s. at*a*khsh*a*iy, 3. s. at*a*khsh*a*ta, 3. p. at*a*khsha(n)ta.

T*a*r, cross.
Impf. 1 s. at*a*ra(m?) (Bh. V, 4) 3. s., at*a*ra (tartiyana?), 1. p. at*a*rayama; Part. t*a*rt*a*.

Tars, fear.
Pres. 3. s. tarsatiy; Impf, 1. s. atarsam, 3. s. atarsa.

Thad, go.(?)
Impf. 2. s. athadaya.

Thah, say.
Pres. 2. s. thahy, 3. s. thatiy, 1. p, (passive) thahyamahy; Impf. 1, s. athaham, 3. s. athaha; Aor. (passive) 3. s. athahi; Inf. thastanaiy.

Trar, guard.
Impf. 1. s. atrarayam.

Dan, flow.
Pres. 3. s. danauvatiy.

Dar, hold.
Pres. 1. s. darayamiy; Impf. 3. s. adaraya; Aor. (passive) 3. s. adariy (adary, adari).

Darsh, dare.
Pres. (middle) 1. s, darshaiy; Impf. 3. s. adarshnaush.

1. Da, know.
Impf. 3, s. adana.

2. Da, put.
Impf. 3. s. adada; Aor. 3. s. ada, adada.

3. Da, give.
Pres. 3. s. dadatuv (impv,)

1. Di, see.
Pres, 2. s. didiy (impv.)

2. Di, take.
Impf. 1. s. adinam, 3. s. adina; Part. dita.

Duruj, deceive.
Pres. 2. s. durujiyahy (subj.;) Impf. 3. s. adurujiya, 3. p. adurujiyasha(n); Part. durukhta.

Duvar, make. (?)
Part. duvarta.

Ni, lead.
Impf. 1. s. anayam, 3. s. anaya, 3. s. (middle) anayata.

Pat, fall.
Impf. 3. s. (middle) apatata.

Pars, examine.
Pres. 2. s. parsahy (subj.) 3. s. parsatiy (subj.) parsa (impv.); Impf. 1. s. aparsam; Part. frasta.

Pa, protect.
Pres. 2. s. padiy (impv.), 3. s. patuv (impv,,) 2. s. (middle) payauva (impv.) Part. pata.

Pish, rub.
Impf. I. s. apisham; Inf. pishtanaiy; Part. pishta.

Ba(n)d, bind.
Part. basta.

Bar, bear.
Pres. 3. p. bara(n)tiy, baratya?, 3. s. baratuv (impv.); Impf. 1. s. abaram, 3. s. abara 3. p. abara(n), 3. p. (middle) abara(n)ta; Part. barta.

Bu, be.
Pres. 3. s. bavatiy (subj.); Impf. 1. s. abavam, 3. s. abava, 3. p. abava(n); Aor. 3. s. biya (Opt.)

Man, think.
Pres. 3. s. maniyatiy (subj.)

Man, remain.
Impf. 3. s. amanaya.

Mar, die.
Impf. (middle) 3. s. amariyata.

Ma, measure.
Part. mata.

Rad, leave.(?)
Impf. 2. s. arada.

Ras, come.
Pres, 3. s. rasatiy (subj.); Impf. 1. s. arasam, 3. s. arasa.

Vain, see.
Pres. 2. s. vainahy (subj.) 3. s. (middle) vainataiy; Impf. 3. s. avaina.

Vaj, lead.
Impf. 1. s. avajam.

Var, cause to believe.
Pres. 3. s. varnavatiy (subj.) 3. s. (middle) varnavatam (impv.)

San, destroy.
Pres. 2. s. sanahy (subj.)

Sar, kill.(?)
Impf. (middle) 3. s. asariyata.

Star, sin.
Impf. 2. s. astarava.

Sta, stand.
Impf. 3. s. aishtata, 1. s. astayam, 3. s. astaya.

Shiyu, go.
Impf. 1. s. ashiyavam, 3. s. ashiyava, 3. p. ashiyava(n).

Ha(n)j, throw.
Impf. 1. s. aha(n)jam.

Had, sit.
Impf. 1. s. ahadayam.

TRANSLITERATION

OF

THE INSCRIPTIONS.

I.

INSCRIPTION OF CYRUS.

INSCRIPTION OF MURGHAB. (M.)

¹Adam ²Kurush ³khshay*a*thiya ⁴H*a*khamanishiy*a*.

---

¹Ad*a*m, 20.   ²Kurush, 16.   ³khshay*a*thiy*a*, 18.   ⁴H*a*kham*a*ni-shiy*a*, 58.

II.

INSCRIPTIONS OF DARIUS HYSTASPES.

THE INSCRIPTION OF BEHISTAN. (BH.)

1. Adam Darayava(h)ush* khshayathiya vazraka khshayathiya khshayathiyanam khshayathiya Parsaiy khshayathiya ¹dahyunam V(i)shthaspahya putra Arshamahya ²napa Hakhamanishiya. 2. ³Thatiy Darayava(h)ush khshayathiya mana ⁴pita V(i)shtaspa V(i)shtaspahya pita Arshama Arshamahya pita Ariyaramna Ariyaramnahya pita [Caishpish] ⁵Caishpaish pita Hakhamanish. 3. Thatiy Darayava(h)ush khshayathiya avahyaradiy vayam Hakhamanishiya ⁶thahyamahy haca ⁷paruviyata ⁸amata ⁹amahy haca paruviyata ¹⁰hya amakham ¹¹tauma khshayathiya aha(n). 4. Thatiy Darayava(h)ush khshayathiya VIII mana taumaya tyaiy paruvam khshayathiya aha(n) adam navama IX duvitatarnam vayam khshayathiya amahy, 5. Thatiy Darayava(h)ush khshayathiya vashna ¹²Auramazdaha adam khshayathiya amiy Auramazda khshatram ¹³mana frabara. 6. Thatiy Darayava(h)ush khshayathiya ¹⁴ima dahyava tya mana ¹⁵patiyaisha(n) vashna Auramazdaha ¹⁶adamsham khshayathiya aham Parsa (H)uvaja Babirush Athura

---

*The author not feeling ready to accept the theory of Linder (Literar. Centralblatt, 1880, p. 358) respecting the derivation of the second member of the compound (cf. Spiegel: Die Altpersischen Keilinschriften, 2nd edition) retained the old spelling +vush in his first edition. The otherwise anomalous genitive +vahaush has induced him to transliterate +va(h)ush. See vocabulary.

¹dahyunam, 21. ²napa, 23. ³thatiy, 15; 39, V. ⁴pita, 22. ⁵Caishpaish, 20. ⁶thahyamahy, 45, B. ⁷paruviyata, 58. ⁸amata, 95, D. ⁹amahy 40 (end)· ¹⁰hya, 30; 87, A. ¹¹tauma, 21. ¹²Auramazdaha, 19. ¹³mana, 83. ¹⁴ima, 28. ¹⁵patiyaisha(n), 48. ¹⁶adamsham, 29.

Arabaya Mudraya tyaiy darayahya Sparda Yauna
Mada Armina Katapatuka Parthava Zara(n)ka Haraiva
Uvarazamiya Bakhtrish Suguda Ga(n)dara Saka
Thatagush Harauvatish Maka fraharvam dahyava
XXIII. 7. Thatiy Darayava(h)ush khshayathiya
ima dahyava tya mana patiyaisha(n) vashna Auramazdaha
mana ba(n)daka aha(n)ta mana 'bajim ²abara(n)ta
tyasham hacama athahy khshapava raucapativa
³ava ⁴akunavyata. 8. Thatiy Darayava(h)ush
khshayathiya a(n)tar ima dahyava martiya hya agata
aha avam ⁵(h)ubartam abaram hya arika aha avam
(h)ufrastam aparsam vashna Auramazdaha ima dahyava
tyana mana data apariyaya(n) yathasham hacama
⁶athahy avatha ⁷akunavyata. 9. Thatiy Darayava(h)ush
khshayathiya Auramazda mana khshatram
frabara Auramazdamaiy upastam ⁸abara ⁹yata ima
khshatram ¹⁰adary vashna Auramazdaha ima khshatram
¹¹darayamiy. 10. Thatiy Darayava(h)ush
khshayathiya ima tya mana ¹²kartam pasava yatha
khshayathiya abavam Ka(m)bujiya nama Kuraush
putra amakham taumaya ¹³hauv paruvam ida khshayathiya
aha avahya Ka(m)bujiyahya brata Bardiya ¹⁴nama
aha hamata hamapita Ka(m)bujiyahya pasava Ka(m)bujiya
avam Bardiyam ¹⁵avaja yatha Ka(m)bujiya
Bardiyam avaja karahya naiy azda abava tya Bardiya
avajata pasava Ka(m)bujiya Mudrayam ashiyava
yatha Ka(m)bujiya Mudrayam ashiyava pasava kara
arika abava pasava drauga dahyauva vasiy abava uta
Parsaiy uta Madaiy uta aniyauva dahyushuva.
11. Thatiy Darayava(h)ush khshayathiya pasava I
martiya Magush aha Gaumata nama hauv udapatata
haca Paishiyauvadaya Arakadrish nama kaufa haca

---

¹ bajim, 20. ² abara(n)ta, 44, 2. ³ ava, 27. ⁴ akunavyata, 45, N. 3. ⁵ (h)ubartam, 04, в. ⁶ athahy, 45, N. 4; 50, N. ⁷ akunavyata, 42. ⁸ abara, 44. ⁹ yata, 95. ¹⁰ adary, 50. ¹¹ darayamiy, 46. ¹² kartam, 53. ¹³ hauv, 28. ¹⁴ nama, 23, в. ¹⁵ avaja, 4, a.

avadasha Viy*a*khn*a*hy*a* mahya XIV ¹r*a*uc*a*bish th*a*kata ah*a* y*a*diy ud*a*y*a*t*a*ta h*a*uv kar*a*hya av*a*tha ²ad*u*rujiya ad*a*m Bardiy*a* amiy hy*a* Kur*a*ush putr*a* K*a*(m)bujiy*a*hya brata pasav*a* kar*a* h*a*ruv*a* h*a*mitriy*a* abav*a* h*a*ca K*a*(m)bujiya abiy av*a*m ashiy*a*v*a* uta Pars*a* uta Mada uta aniya d*a*hyav*a* khsh*a*tr*a*m h*a*uv ag*a*rbay*a*ta Garm*a*pad*a*hy*a* mahya IX r*a*uc*a*bish th*a*k*a*ta ah*a* av*a*tha khsh*a*tr*a*m ag*a*rbayata p*a*sav*a* K*a*(m)bujiy*a* (h)uvam*a*rshiyush am*a*riy*a*ta. 12. Thatiy Dar*a*ya-va(h)ush khshayathiy*a* ait*a* khsh*a*tr*a*m ty*a* Gaum*a*ta hy*a* M*a*gush ³adina K*a*(m)bujiy*a*m ait*a* khsh*a*tram h*a*ca p*a*ruviy*a*ta am*a*kh*a*m t*a*um*a*ya ah*a* p*a*sav*a* Gaum*a*ta hya M*a*gush adina K*a*(m)bujiy*a*m uta Pars*a*m uta Mad*a*m uta aniya d*a*hyav*a* h*a*uv ay*a*sta uvaip*a*shiyam akut*a* h*a*uv khshay*a*thiy*a* abav*a*. 13. Thatiy Dar*a*yav*a*(h)ush khshay*a*thiy*a* n*a*iy ah*a* m*a*rtiya n*a*iy Pars*a* n*a*iy Mada n*a*iy am*a*kh*a*m t*a*umaya ⁴k*a*shciy hy*a* avam Gaumat*a*m ty*a*m M*a*gum khsh*a*tr*a*m dit*a*m ⁵c*a*khriya kar*a*shim h*a*ca d*a*rsh*a*m*a* at*a*rs*a* kar*a*m v*a*siy avaj*a*niya hy*a* par*a*n*a*m Bardiy*a*m adana av*a*hy*a*radiy kar*a*m avaj*a*niya ⁶maty*a*mam khshnasatiy ty*a* ad*a*m n*a*iy Bardiy*a* amiy hy*a* Kur*a*ush putr*a* k*a*shciy n*a*iy ad*a*rshn*a*ush cishciy th*a*st*a*n*a*iy p*a*riy Gaumat*a*m ty*a*m M*a*gum yata ad*a*m ar*a*s*a*m p*a*sav*a* ad*a*m Aur*a*m*a*zdam p*a*tiyavah*a*iy Auramazdam*a*iy up*a*stam ab*a*r*a* Baga-yad*a*ish mahya X r*a*uc*a*bish th*a*k*a*ta ah*a* av*a*tha ad*a*m h*a*da kam*a*n*a*ibish m*a*rtiy*a*ibish av*a*m Gaumat*a*m ty*a*m M*a*gum avaj*a*n*a*m uta ty*a*ish*a*iy frat*a*ma m*a*rtiya anushiya ah*a*(n)ta Sik*a*y*a*uv*a*tish ⁷n*a*ma* dida Nisay*a* nama d*a*hyaush Mad*a*iy avad*a*shim avaj*a*n*a*m ⁸khsh*a*tramshim adam adin*a*m vashna Aur*a*m*a*zdah*a* ad*a*m

*For forms nam*a* and nama cf. the Grammar; but see Bartholomae, Arische Forsch. I, 58; also Thumb, Zeitsch. für vergl. Sprachforsch. (1891)

¹ r*a*uc*a*bish, 23.   ²adurujiy*a*, 45.   ³adina, 43.   ⁴k*a*shciy, 31.
⁵c*a*khriya, 47.   ⁶maty*a*mam, 101, A.   ⁷nama, 24; 61, A. Note 2.
⁸khsh*a*tr*a*mshim ad*a*m adin*a*m, 64.

khshayathiya abavam Auramazda khshatram mana frabara. 14. Thatiy Darayava(h)ush khshayathiya khshatram tya 'haca amakham taumaya parabartam aha ava adam patipadam akunavam adamshim *gathva* avastayam yatha paruvamciy avatha adam akunavam ayadana tya Gaumata hya Magush viyaka adam niyatrarayam karahya abacarish gaithamca maniyamca ³v(i)thibishca tyadish Gaumata hya Magush adina adam karam gathva avastayam Parsamca Madamca uta aniya dahyava yatha paruvamciy avatha adam tya parabartam patiyabaram vashna Auramazdaha ima adam akunavam adam hamatakhshaiy yata v(i)tham tyam amakham gathva avastayam yatha paruvamciy avatha adam hamatakhshaiy vashna Auramazdaha yatha Gaumata hya Magush v(i)tham tyam amakham naiy parabara. 15. Thatiy Darayava(h)ush khshayathiya ima tya adam akunavam pasava yatha khshayathiya abavam. 16. Thatiy Darayava(h)ush khshayathiya yatha adam Gaumatam tyam Magum avajanam pasava I martiya Atrina nama Upadara(n)mahya putra hauv udapatata (H)uvajaiy karahya avatha athaha adam (H)uvajaiy khshayathiya amiy pasava (H)uvajiya hamitriya abava(n) abiy avam Atrinam ashiyava(n) hauv khshayathiya abava (H)uvajaiy uta I martiya Babiruviya Naditabira nama Aina - - hya putra hauv udapatata Babirauv karam avatha adurujiya adam Nabuk(u)dracara amiy hya Nabunitahya putra pasava kara hya Babiruviya haruva abiy avam Naditabiram ashiyava Babirush hamitriya abava khshatram tya Babirauv hauv agarbayata. 17. Thatiy Darayava(h)ush khshayathiya pasava adam (karam) ⁴fraishayam

---

* It is possible to regard this form as a locative (gathava) with postpositive a (cf. note on (H)ufratauva I, 19; but the instrumental seems preferable).

¹ haca amakham taumaya, 76. ² gathva, 73. ³ v(i)thibishca, 70, A.
⁴ fraishayam (H)uvajam, 66.

(H)uvajam hauv Atrina basta anayata abiy mam
adamshim avajanam. 18. Thatiy Darayava(h)ush
khshayathiya pasava adam Babirum ashiyavam abiy
avam Naditabiram hya ¹Nabuk(u)dracara agaubata
kara hya Naditabirahya Tigram adarayaJaishtata uta
abish naviya aha pasava adam karam-makauva ava-
kanam aniyam dashabarim akunavam aniyahya ashm
... anayam Auramazdamaiy upastam abara vashna
Auramazdaha Tigram viyatarayama avada karam
tyam Naditabirahya adam ajanam vasiy Atriyadiyahya mahya ²XXVII raucabish thakata aha avatha
hamaranam akuma. 19. Thatiy Darayava(h)ush
khshayathiya pasava adam Babirum ashiyavam athiy
Babirum yatha - - - - - - - - ayam Zazana nama vardanam ³anuv (H)ufratauva* avada hauv Naditabira hya
Nabuk(u)dracara agaubata aisha ⁴hada kara ⁵patish
mam hamaranam cartanaiy pasava hamaranam akuma
Auramazdamaiy upastam abara vashna Auramazdaha
karam tyam Naditabirahya adam ajanam vasiy aniya
apiya - h - - a . . apishim parabara Anamakahya
mahya ⁶II raucabish thakata aha avatha hamaranam
akuma.

---

*(H)ufratauva: The a which occurs at the end of this locative termination is doubtless the prefix a of the Sanskrit. For a full discussion of this postpositive a; cf. Bezzenbergers Beiträge, XIII; also for the same postpositive a in Avestan, cf Jackson Am. Or. Society Proceedings (1889) and Kuhns Zeitschrift, XXXI. Cf. Grammar, 16, F.

¹ Nabuk(u)dracara agaubata, 61, B. ² XXVII raucabish, 72.
³ anuv (H)ufratauva, 84. ⁴ hada kara, 70. ⁵ patish mam - catanaiy,
54. N.; 60, B; 04. ⁶ II raucabish, 60, C.

II.

1. Thatiy Darayava(h)ush hkshayathiya pasava Naditabira hada kamanaibish asbaribish abiy Babirum ashiyava pasava adam Babirum ashiyavam vashna Auramazdaha uta Babirum agarbayam uta avam Naditabiram agarbayam pasava avam Naditabiram adam Babirauv avajanam. 2. Thatiy Darayava(h)ush khshayathiya yata adam Babirauv aham ima dahyava tya hacama hamitriya abava(n) Parsa (H)uvaja Mada Athura Armina Parthava Margush Thatagush Saka. 3. Thatiy Darayava(h)ush khshayathiya I martiya Martiya nama Cicikhraish putra ¹Kuganaka nama vardanam Parsaiy avada adaraya hauv udapatata (H)uvajaiy karahya avatha athaha adam Imanish amiy (H)uvajaiy khshayathiya. 4. Thatiy Darayava(h)ush khshayathiya adakaiy adam ashnaiy aham abiy (H)uvajam pasava hacama - - - - (H)uvajiya avam Mattiyam agarbaya(n) hyasham mathishta aha utashim avajana(n). 5. Thatiy Darayava(h)ush khshayathiya I martiya Fravartish nama Mada hauv udapatata Maldaiy karahya avatha athaha adam Khshathrita amiy (H)uvakhshatarahya taumaya pasava kara Mada hya v(i)thapatiy aha hacama hamitriya abava abiy avam Fravartim ashiyava hauv khshayathiya abava Madaiy. 6. Thatiy Darayava(h)ush khshayathiya kara Parsa uta Mada hya upa mam aha *hauv kamanam aha pasava adam karam fraishayam Vidarna nama Parsa mana ba(n)daka avamsham mathishtam akunavam avathasham athaham paraita avam karam tyam Madam jata hya mana naiy gaubataiy pasava hauv Vidarna hada kara ashiyava yatha Madam pararasa Ma ... nama vardanam Madaiy avada hamaranam akunaush hada Madaibish hya Madaishuva mathishta aha hauv adakaiy kamanamciy naiy adaraya Auramazdamaiy upastam abara

---
¹ Kuganaka nama, 61 A, Note 2.   ² hauv kamanam-aha, 80 A.

vashna Auramazdaha kara hya Vidarnahya avam
karam tyam hamitriyam aja vasiy Anamakahya
mahya VI raucabish thakata aha ¹avathasham hamaranam kartam pasava hauv kara hya mana Ka(m)-
pada nama dahyaush Madaiy avada mam cita amanaya yata adam arasam Madam. **7.** Thatiy Dara-
yava(h)ush khshayathiya pasava Dadarshish nama
Arminiya mana ba(n)daka avam adam fraishayam
Arminam avathashaiy athaham paraidiy kara hya
hamitriya mana naiy gaubataiy avam jadiy pasava
Dadarshish ashiyava yatha Arminam pararasa pasava
hamitriya ²ha(n)gmata paraita patish Dadarhim hamaranam cartanaiy ..... nama avahanam Armaniyaiy avada hamaranam akunava(n) Auramazdamaiy
upastam abara vashna Auramazdaha kara hya mana
avam karam tyam hamitriyam.. aja vasiy Thuravaharahya mahya VI raucabish thakata aha avathasham
hamaranam kartam. **8.** Thatiy Darayava(h)ush
khshayathiya patiy duvitiyam hamitriya ha(n)gmata
paraita patish Dadarshim hamaranam cartanaiy Tigra
nama dida Armaniyaiy avada hamaranam akunava(n)
Auramazdamaiy upastam abara vashna Auramazdaha
kara hya mana avam karam tyam hamitriyam aja
vasiy Thuravaharahya mahya XVIII raucabish thakata aha avathasham hamaranam kartam. **9.** Thatiy Darayava(h)ush khshayathiya patiy tritiyam
hamitriya ha(n)gmata paraita patish Dadarshim hamaranam cartanaiy U .... ama nama dida Armaniyaiy avada hamaranam akunava(n) Auramazdamaiy
upastam abara vashna Auramazdaha kara hya mana
avam karam tyam hamitriyam aja vasiy Thaigarcaish
mahya IX raucabish thakata aha avathasham hamaranam kartam pasava Dadarshish cita mam amanaya
. a ... yata adam arasam Madam. **10.** Thatiy Dara-
yava(h)ush khshayathiya pasava Vaumisa nama

---

¹ avathasham, 60, c.   ² ha(n)gmata, 89, c.

Parsa mana ba(n)daka avam adam fraishayam Arminam avathashaiy athaham paraidiy kara hya hamitriya mana naiy gaubataiy avam jadiy pasava Vaumisa ashiyava yatha Arminam pararasa pasava hamitriya ha(n)gmata paraita patish Vaumisam hamaranam cartanaiy -- I --- nama dahyaush Athuraya avada hamaranam akunava(n) Auramazdamaiy upastam abara vashna Auramazdaha kara hya mana avam karam tyam hamitriyam aja vasiy Anamakahya mahya XV raucabish thakata aha avathasham hamaranam kartam. **11.** Thatiy Darayava(h)ush khshayathiya patiy duvitiyam hamitriya ha(n)gmata paraita patish Vaumisam hamaranam cartanaiy Autiyara nama dahyaush Arminaiy avada hamaranam akunava(n) Auramazdamaiy upastam abarḍ vashna Auramazdaha kara hya mana avam karam tyam hamitriyam aja vasiy Thuravaharahya mahya - iyamanam patiy avathasham hamaranam kartam pasava Vaumisa cita mam amanaya Arminaiy yata adam arasam Madam. **12.** Thatiy Darayava(h)ush khshayathiya pasava adam nijayam haca Babiraush ashiyavam Madam yatha Madam pararasam Kud(u)rush nama vardanam Madaiy avada hauv Fravartish hya Madaiy khshayathiya agaubata aisha hada kara patish mam hamaranam cartanaiy pasava hamaranam akuma Auramazdamaiy upastam abara vashna Auramazdaha karam tyam Fravartaish adam ajanam vasiy Adukanaish mahya XXVI raucabish thakata aha avatha hamaranam akuma. **13.** Thatiy Darayava(h)ush khshayathiya pasava hauv Fravartish hada hamanaibish asbaribish amutha Raga nama dahyaush Madaiy avada ashiyava pasava adam karam fraishayam ¹tyaipatiy Fravartish ²agarbayata anayata abiy mam adamshaiy uta naham uta gausha uta izavam frajanam utashaiy - - - ma avajam duvarayamaiy

---

¹ tyaipatiy, 88, B. ² agarbayata anayata, 89, B.

basta adariy haruvashim kara avaina pasava adam Ha(n)gmatanaiy uzamayapatiy akunavam uta martiya tyaishaiy fratama anushiya aha(n)ta avaiy Ha(n)gmatanaiy a(n)tar didam fraha(n)jam. 14. Thatiy Darayava(h)ush khshayathiya I martiya Citra(n)takhma nama Asagartiya hauvmaiy hamitriya abava karahya avatha athaha adam khshayathiya amiy Asagartaiy (H)uvakhshatarahya taumaya pasava adam karam Parsam uta Madam fraishayam Takhmaspada nama Mada mana ba(n)daka avamsham mathishtam akunavam avathasham athaham paraita karam tyam hamitriyam hya mana naiy gaubataiy avam jata pasava Takhmaspada hada kara ashiyava hamaranam akunaush hada Citra(n)takhma Auramazdamaiy upastam abara vashna Auramazdaha kara hya mana avam karam tyam hamitriyam aja uta Citra(n)takhmam agarbaya anaya abiy mam pasavashaiy adam uta naham uta gausha frajanam utashaiy - - shma avajam duvarayamaiy basta adariy haruvashim kara avaina pasavashim Arbiraya uzamayapatiy akunavam. 15. Thatiy Darayava(h)ush khshayathiya ima tya mana kartam Madaiy. 16. Thatiy Darayava(h)ush khshayathiya Parthava uta Varkana - - - - - va - - - - - Fravartaish - - - - agaubata V(i)shtaspa mana pita h - - - - kara avahar - - - - atara pasava V(i)shtaspa ab - - - - - anushiya - - - aya Vispauz - - tish nama vardanam - - - - - da hamaranam akunava - - - - - - - - - - - - avathasham hamaranam kartam.

III.

1. Thatiy Darayava(h)ush khshayathiya pasava adamkaram Parsam fraishayam abiy V(i)shtaspam haca Ragaya yatha hauv kara pararasa abiy V(i)shtaspam pasava V(i)shtaspa ayasta avam karam ashiyava Patigrabana nama vardanam Parthavaiy avada hamaranam akunaush hada hamitriyaibish Auramazdamaiy upastam abara vashna Auramazdaha V(i)shtaspa avam karam tyam hamitriyam aja vasiy Garmapadahya mahya ¹I rauca thakata aha avathasham hamaranam kartam. 2. Thatiy Darayava(h)ush khshayathiya yasava dahyaush mana abava ima tya mana kartam Parthavaiy. 3. Thatiy Darayava(h)ush khshayathiya Margush nama dahyaush hauvmaiy hashitiya abava ²I martiya Frada nama Margava avam mathishtam akunava(n)ta pasava adam ³fraishayam Dadarshish nama Parsa mana ba(n)daka Bakhtriya khshatrapava abiy avam avathashaiy athaham paraidiy avam karam jadiy hya mana naiy gaubataiy pasava Dadarshish hada kara ashiyava hamaranam akunaush hada Margayaibish Auramazdamaiy upastam abara vashna Auramazdaha kara hya mana avam karam .. tyam hamitriyam aja vasiy Atriyadiyahya mahya XXIII raucabish thakata aha avathasham hamaranam kartam. 4. Thatiy Darayava(h)ush khshayathiya pasava dahyaush mana abava ima tya mana kartam Bakhtriya. 5. Thatiy Darayava(h)ush khshayathiya I martiya Vahyazdata nama Tarava nama vardanam Yutiya nama dahyaush Parsaiy avada adaraya hauv duvitiyam udapatata Parsaiy karahya avatha athaha adam Bardiya amiy hya Kuraush putra pasava kara Parsa hya v(i)thapatiy haca yadaya fratarta hauv hacama hamitriya abava abiy avam Vahyazdatam ashiyava hauv khshayathiya abava Parsaiy. 6. Tha-

---
¹ I rauca, 46, A. ² I martiya Frada – avam, 61, A. ³ fraishayam Dadarshish, 61, A, Note 1.

tiy Darayava(h)ush khshayathiya pasava adam karam
Parsam uta Madam fraishayam hya upa mam aha
Artavardiya nama Parsa mana ba(n)daka avamsham
mathishtam akunavam hya aniya kara Parsa ¹pasa
mana ashiyava Madam pasava Artavardiya hada kara
ashiyava Parsam yatha Parsam pararasa Rakha nama
vardanam Parsaiy avada hauv Vahyazdata hya Bardiya agaubata aisha hada kara patish Artavardiyam
hamaranam cartanaiy pasava hamaranam akunava(n)
Auramazdamaiy upastam abara vashna Auramazdaha
kara hya mana avam karam tyam Vahyazdatahya
aja vasiy Thuravaharahya mahya XII raucabish thakata aha avathasham hamaranam kartam. 7. Thatiy
Darayava(h)ush khshayathiya pasava hauv Vahyazdata hada kamanaibish asabaribish amutha ashiyava
Paishiyauvadam haca avadasha karam ayasta hyaparam aisha patish Artavardiyam hamaranam cartanaiy
Paraga nama kaufa avada hamaranam akunava(n)
Auramazdamaiy upastam abara vashna Auramazdaha
kara hya mana avam karam tyam Vahyazdatahya
aja vasiy Garmapadahya mahya VI raucabish thakata
aha avathasham hamaranam kartam uta avam Vahyazdatam agarbaya(n) uta martiya tyaishaiy fratama
anushiya aha(n)ta agarbaya(n). 8. Thatiy Daraya-
va(h)ush khshayathiya pasava adam avam Vahyazdatam uta martiya tyaishaiy fratama anushiya
aha(n)ta Uvadaidaya nama vardanam Parsaiy ava-
dashish uzamayapatiy akunavam. 9. Thatiy Dara-
yava(h)ush khshayathiya hauv Vahyazdata hya Bardiya agaubata hauv karam fraishaya Harauvatim
Vivana nama Parsa mana ba(n)daka Harauvatiya
khshatrapava abiy avam utasham I martiyam mathishtam akunaush avathasham athaha paraita Vivanam jata uta avam karam hya Darayavahush
khshayathiyahya gaubataiy pasava hauv kara ashiya-

---

¹ pasa mana, 80, в.

va tyam Vahyazdata fraishaya abiy Vivanam hamaranam cartanaiy Kapishakanish nama dida avada hamaranam akunava(n) Auramazdamaiy upastam abara vashna Auramazdaha kara hya mana avam karam tyam hamitriyam aja vasiy Anamakahya mahya XIII raucabish thakata aha ¹avathasham hamaranam kartam. **10.** Thatiy Darayava(h)ush khshayathiya patiy hyaparam hamitriya ha(n)gmata paraita patish Vivanam hamaranam cartanaiy Ga(n)dutava nama dahyaush avada hamaranam akunava(n) Auramazdamaiy upastam abara vashna Auramazdaha kara hya mana avam karam tyam hamitriyam aja vasiy Viyakhnahya mahya VII raucabish thakata aha avathasham hamaranam kartam. **11.** Thatiy Darayava(h)ush khshayathiya pasava hauv martiya hya avahya karahya mathishta aha tyam Vahyazdata fraishaya abiy Vivanam hauv mathishta hada kamanaibish asabaribish ashiyava Arshada nama dida Harauvatiya avapara atiyaisha pasava Vivana hada kara ²nipadiy tyaiy ashiyava avadashim agarbaya uta martiya tyaishaiy fratama anushiya aha(n)ta avaja. **12.** Thatiy Darayava(h)ush khshayathiya pasava dahyaush mana abava ima tya mana kartam Harauvatiya. **13.** Thatiy Darayava(h)ush khshayathiya yata adam Parsaiy uta Madaiy aham patiy duvitiyam Babiruviya hamitriya abava(n) hacama I martiya Arakha nama Arminiya Han(?)ditahya putra hauv udapatata Babirauv Duban(?)a nama dahyaush haca avadasha hauv udapatata avatha adurujiya adam Nabukudracara amiy hya Nabunitahya putra pasava kara Babiruyiya hacama hamitriya abava abiy avam Arakham ashiyava Babirum hauv agarbayata hauv khshayathiya abava Babirauv. **14.** Thatiy Darayava(h)ush khshayathiya pasava adam karam fraishayam Babirum Vi(n)dafra nama Mada mana ba(n)daka

---

¹ avathasham hamaranam kartam, 80, A. ² nipadiy, 84, A.

avam mathishtam akunavam avathasham athaham paraita avam karam tyam Babirauv jata hya mana naiy gaubataiy pasava Vi(n)dafra hada kara ashiyava abiy Babirum Auramzdamaiy upastam abara vashna Auramazdaha Vi(n)dafra βabirum agarbaya - - - - - mahya II raucabish thakata aha avatha ava - - - - - - - - - -
- - - - - - - - - apatiy asariyata.

IV.

1. Thatiy Daraya̯va(h)ush khshayathiya ima tya mana kartam Babirauv. 2. Thatiy Daraya̯va(h)ush khshayathiya ima tya adam akunavam vashna Auramazdaha aha hamahyaya tharda pasava yatha khshayathiya hamitriya abava(n) adam XIX hamarana akunavam vashna Auramazdaha 'adamsham ajanam uta IX khshayathiya agarbayam I Gaumata nama Magush aha hauv adurujiya avatha athaha adam Bardiya amiy hya Kuraush putra hauv Parsam hamitriyam akunaush 1 Atrina nama (H)uvajaiy hauv adurujiya avatha athaha adam khshayathiya amiy (H)uvajaiy hauv (H)uvajam hamitriyam akunaush mana I Naditabira nama Babiruviya hauv adurujiya avatha athaha adam Nabukudracara amiy hya Nabunitahya putra hauv Babirum hamitriyam akunaush I Martiya nama Parsa hauv adurujiya avatha athaha adam Imanish amiy (H)uvajaiy khshayathiya hauv (H)uvajam hamitriyam akunaush I Fravartish nama Mada hauv adurujiya avatha athaha adam Khshathrita amiy (H)uvakhshatarahya taumaya hauv Madam hamitriyam akunaush I Citra(n)takhma nama Asagartiya hauv adurujiya avatha athaha adam khshayathiya amiy Asagartaiy (H)uvakhshatarahya taumaya hauv Asagartam hamitriyam akunaush I Frada nama Margava hauv adurujiya avatha athaha adam khshayathiya amiy Margauv hauv Margum hamitriyam akunaush I Vahyazdata nama Parsa hauv adurujiya avatha athaha adam Bardiya amiy Kuraush putra hauv Parsam hamitriyam akunaush I Arakha nama Arminiya hauv adurujiya avatha athaha adam Nabukudracara amiy hya Nabunitahya putra hauv Babirum hamitriyam akunaush. 3. Thatiy Darayava(h)ush khshayathiya imaiy IX khshayathiya adam agarbayam a(n)tar ima hamarana. 4. Thatiy Dara-

---
[1] adamsham ajanam, 83, B.

yava(h)ush khshayathiya dahyava ima tya hamitriya abava(n) draugadish akunaush ¹tya imaiy karam adurujiyasha(n) pasava dish Auramazda mana dastaya akunaush yatha ²mam kama avatha di - -. 5. Thatiy Darayava(h)ush khshayathiya tuvam ka khshayathiya hya aparam ahy ³haca drauga darsham patipayauva martiya hya draujana ahatiy avam (h)ufrastam parsa yadiy avatha ⁴maniyahy dahyaushmaiy duruva ahatiy. 6. Thatiy Darayava(h)ush khshayathiya ima tya adam akunavam vashna Auramazdaha ⁵hamahyaya tharda akunavam tuvam ka hya aparam imam dipim ⁶patiparsahy tya mana kartam varnavatam ⁷thuvam matya durujiyahy. 7. Thatiy Darayava-(h)ush khshayathiya Auramazda taiyiya yatha ima hashiyam naiy durukhtam adam akunavam hamahyaya tharda. 8. Thatiy Darayava(h)ush khshayathiya vashna Auramazdaha - - amaiy aniyashciy vasiy astiy kartam ava ahyaya dipiya naiy nipishtam avahyaradiy naiy nipishtam matya hya aparam imam dipim patiparsatiy avahya paruv tha .... tya mana kartam naishim varnavatiy durukhtam maniyatiy. 9. Thatiy Darayava(h)ush khshayathiya tyaiy paruva khshayathiya - a aha(n) avaisham naiy astiy kartam yatha mana vashna Auramazdaha hamahyaya duvartam. 10. Thatiy Darayava(h)ush khshayathiya - - - nuram thuvam varnavatam tya mana kartam avatha - - - avahyaradiy ma apagaudaya yadiy imam ha(n)dugam naiy apagaudayahy karahya thahy Auramazda thuvam daushta ⁸biya utataiy tauma vasiy biya uta dra(n)gam jiva. 11. Thatiy Darayava(h)ush khshayathiya yadiy imam ha(n)dugam apagaudayahy naiy thahy karahya Auramazdatay jata biya utataiy tauma ma biya. 12. Thatiy Darayava(h)ush khshayathiya ima tya adam akunavam hamahyaya tharda

---

¹ tya imaiy karam adurujiyasha(n), 07. ² mam kama, 66. ³ haca drauga, 77. ⁴ maniyahy, 91, A. ⁵ hamahyaya tharda, 80, c. ⁶ patiparsahy, 91. ⁷ thuvam matya durujiyahy, 89, A. ⁸ biya, 51, N.

vashna Auramazdaha akunavam Auramazdamaiy upastam abara uta aniya bagaha tyaiy ha(n)tiy. 13. Thatiy Darayava(h)ush khshayathiya avahyaradiy Auramazda upastam abara uta aniya bagaha tyaiy ha(n)tiy yatha naiy arika aham naiy draujana aham naiy zurakara aham - - - - - imaiy tauma upariy abashtam upariy mam naiy shakaurim - - - - - huvatam zura akunavam tyamaiy hya hamatakhshata mana vithiya avam (h)ubartam abaram hya iyani.. avam (h)ufrastam aparsam. 14. Thatiy Darayava(h)ush khshayathiya ¹tuvam ka khshayathiya hya aparam ahy martiya hya draujana ahatiy hyava - tar - - - ahatiy avaiy ma daushta avaiy ahifrashtadiy parsa. 15. Thatiy Darayava(h)ush khshayathiya tuvam ka hya aparam imam dipim vainahy tyam adam niyapisham imaiva patikara matya ²visanahy yava jivahy ava(?) avatha parikara. 16. Thatiy Darayava(h)ush khshayathiya yadiy imam dipim vainahy imaiva patikara naiydish visanahy utamaiy ³yava tauma ahatiy parikarahadish Auramazda ⁴thuvam daushta biya utataiy tauma vasiy biya uta dra(n)gam jiva uta tya kunavahy avataiy Auramazda m - - - m jadanautuv. 17. Thatiy Darayava(h)ush khshayathiya yadiy imam dipim imaiva patikara vainahy visanahadish utamaiy yava tauma ahatiy naiydish parikarahy Auramazdataiy jata biya utataiy tauma ma biya uta tya kunavahy avataiy Auramazda nika(n)tuv. 18. Thatiy Darayava(h)ush khshayathiya imaiy martiya tyaiy adakaiy avada aha(n)ta yata adam Gaumatam tyam Magum avajanam hya Bardiya agaubata adakaiy imaiy martiya hamatakhsha(n)ta anushiya mana Vi(n)dafrana nama Vayasparahya putra Parsa Utana nama Thukhrahya putra Parsa Gaubaruva nama Marduniyahya putra Parsa Vidarna nama Bagabignahya

---

¹ tuvam ka, 62. ² visanahy, 91, D. ³ yava tauma ahatiy, 91, g.
⁴ thuvam daushta biya, 65.

putra Parsa Bagabukhsha nama Daduhyahya putra
Parsa Ardumanish nama Vahaukahya putra Parsa.
19. Thatiy Darayava(h)ush khshayathiya tuvam ka
khshayathiya hya aparam ahy tyama vidam tartiyana—tya Darayava(h)ush - - - - - - - - - - -
- - akunavam.

V.

1. Thatiy Darayava(h)ush khshayathiya ima tya adam akunavam ma . r . . . . . . thardam - - tha khshayathiya . . . . vajanam . . . . . . dahyaush hauv hacama hamitriya abava I martiya - imaima nama (H)uvajiya avam mathishtam akunava(n) pasava adam karam fraishayam (H)uvajam I martiya Gaubaruva nama Parsa mana ba(n)daka avamsham mathishtam akunavam pasava hauv Gaubaruva hada kara ashiyava (H)uvajam hamaranam akunaush hada hamitriyaibish pasava . . . . . . utashaiy marda uta . . . . agarbaya uta aniya abiy mam . . . . dahyaush . . . . janam avadashim . . . . 2. Thatiy Darayava(h)ush khshayathiya a . . . uta dah . . . Auramazda . . aya . . . vashna Auramazdaha . . . thadish akunavam. 3. Thatiy Darayava(h)ush khshayathiya hya aparam imam ya . . . . . . hatiy uta jivahya . . . . . . 4. Thatiy Darayava(h)ush khshayathiya . . . . . . ashiyavam abiy Sakam . . . . Tigram baratya . . . . iy abiy darayam avam . . . . a pisa viyatara . . . . ajanam aniyam agarbayam . . . . abiy mam uta . . . . . . Saku(n)ka nama avam agarbayam . . . . avada aniyam mathishtam . . . . am aha pasava da . . . . 5. Thatiy Darayava(h)ush khshayathiya . . . . ma naiy Auramazda . . . . yadiy vashna Auramazdaha . . . . akunavam. 6. Thatiy Darayava(h)ush khshayathiya . . . . . . Auramazdam yadata . . . . uta jivahya uta . .

Smaller Behistan Inscriptions.

a.
OVER THE PICTURE OF DARIUS.

Ad*a*m Dar*a*y*a*v*a*(h)ush khshay*a*thiy*a* v*a*zr*a*k*a* khshay*a*thiy*a* khshay*a*thiyan*a*m khshay*a*thiy*a* Par-s*a*iy khshay*a*thiy*a* d*a*hyunam V(i)shtasp*a*hya putr*a* Arsham*a*hya n*a*pa H*a*kham*a*nishiy*a* Thatiy Dar*a*y*a*v*a*(h)ush khshay*a*thiy*a* m*a*na pita V(i)shtaspa V(i)shtasp*a*hya pita Arsham*a* Arsham*a*hya pita Ariyar*a*mn*a* Ariyar*a*mn*a*hya pita C*a*ishpish C*a*ishp*a*ish pita H*a*kham*a*nish Thatiy Dar*a*yav*a*(h)ush khshay*a*thiy*a* av*a*hy*a*radiy v*a*y*a*m H*a*kham*a*nishiya th*a*hyam*a*hy h*a*ca p*a*ruviy*a*ta amata am*a*hy h*a*ca p*a*ruviy*a*ta hya am*a*kh*a*m t*a*uma khshay*a*thiya ah*a*(n) Thatiy Dar*a*y*a*v*a*(h)ush khshay*a*thiy*a* VIII m*a*na t*a*umaya ty*a*iy p*a*ruv*a*m khshay*a*thiya ah*a*(n) ad*a*m n*a*v*a*m*a* IX duvitat*a*rn*a*m v*a*y*a*m khshay*a*thiya am*a*hy

b.
UNDER THE PROSTRATE FORM.

Iy*a*m G*a*umat*a* hy*a* M*a*gush adurujiy*a* avatha ath*a*ha ad*a*m Bardiy*a* amiy hy*a* Kur*a*ush putr*a* ad*a*m khshay*a*thiya amiy.

c.
OVER THE FIRST UPRIGHT FIGURE.

Iy*a*m Atrin*a* adurujiy*a* av*a*tha ath*a*h*a* ad*a*m khshay*a*thiy*a* amiy (H)uv*a*jaiy.

d.
OVER THE SECOND FIGURE.

Iy*a*m N*a*ditabir*a* adurujiy*a* avatha ath*a*h*a* ad*a*m N*a*buk(u)dr*a*c*a*r*a* amiy hy*a* N*a*bunit*a*hy*a* putr*a* ad*a*m khshay*a*thiya amiy Babir*a*uv.

e.
UPON THE LOWER PART OF THE ATTIRE OF THIRD FIGURE.

Iyam Fravartish adurujiya avatha athaha adam Khshathrita amiy (H)uvakhshayatarahya taumaya adam khshayathiya amiy Madaiy.

f.
OVER THE FOURTH FIGURE.

Iyam Martiya adurujiya avatha athaha adam Imanish amiy (H)uvajaiy khshayathiya.

g.
OVER THE FIFTH FIGURE.

Iyam Citra(n)takhma adurujiya avatha athaha adam khshayathiya Asagartaiy (H)uvakhshatarahya taumaya.

h.
OVER THE SIXTH FIGURE.

Iyam Vahyazdata adurujiya avatha athaha adam Bardiya amiy hya Kuraush putra adam khshayathiya amiy.

i.
OVER THE SEVENTH FIGURE.

Iyam Arakha adurujiya avatha athaha adam Nabuk(u)dracara amiy hya Nabunitahya putra adam khshayathiya amiy Babirauv.

j.
OVER THE EIGHTH FIGURE.

Iyam Frada adurujiya avatha athaha adam khshayathiya amiy Margauv.

k.
OVER THE NINTH FIGURE.

Iyam Saku(n)ka hya Saka.

III.

The Inscription of Alvend. (O.)

B*a*g*a* v*a*zr*a*k*a* Aur*a*m*a*zda hy*a* imam bumim ada hy*a* av*a*m asman*a*m ada hy*a* martiy*a*m ada hy*a* shiyatim ada martiy*a*hya hy*a* [1]Dar*a*y*a*v*a*(h)um khshay*a*thiy*a*m aiv*a*m p*a*runam framatar*a*m Ad*a*m Dar*a*y*a*v*a*(h)ush khshay*a*thiya v*a*zr*a*k*a* khshay*a*thiya khshay*a*thiyanam khshay*a*thiyā d*a*hyunam p*a*ruz*a*nanam khshay*a*thiy*a* ahyaya bumiya v*a*zr*a*kaya dur*a*iy apiy Vishtasp*a*hya putr*a* H*a*kham*a*nishiy*a*.

---

[1] Dar*a*y*a*v*a*(b)um khshay*a*thiy*a*m akun*a*ush, Ū4, A.

IV.

Inscriptions of Suez. (SZ.)

a.

Darayava(h)ush khshayathiya vazraka khshayathiya khshayathiyanam khshayathiya dahyunam Vishtaspahya putra Hakhamanishiya.

b.

Baga vazraka Auramazda hya avam asmanam ada hya imam bumim ada hya martiyam ada hya shiyatim ada martiyahya hya Darayava(h)um khshayathiyam akunaush hya Darayavahaush khshayathiyahya khshatram frabara tya vazrakam tya.... Adam Darayava(h)ush khshayathiya vazraka khshayathiya khshayathiyanam khshayathiya dahyunam paruvzananam khshayathiya ahyaya bumiya vazrakaya duraiy apiy Vishtaspahya putra Hakhamanishiya Thatiy Darayava(h)ush khshayathiya adam Parsa ainiy hada Parsa Mudrayam agarbayam adam niyashtayam imam yuviyam ka(n)tanaiy haca [1]Pirava nama rauta tya Mudrayaiy danauvatiy abiy daraya tya haca Parsa aitiy pasava iyam yuviya (akaniy) ava(da) yatha adam niyashtayam ut......ayata haca...ya mam yuviyam abiy pa......ta yatha ma .....

---
[1] Pirava nama rauta, 68.

V.

Inscription of London.
Adam Darayava(h)ush khshayáthiya.

Inscriptions of Persepolis.

H.
ABOVE THE WALL SURROUNDING THE PALACE OF PERSEPOLIS.

Auramazda vazraka hya mathishta baganam hauv Darayava(h)um khshayathiyam adada haushaiy khshatram frabara vashna Auramazdaha Darayava(h)ush khshayathiya Thatiy Darayava(h)ush khshayathiya iyam dahyaush Parsa tyam mana Auramazdā frabara hya naiba ([h]uvaspa) (h)umartiya vashna Auramazdaha manaca Darayavahaush khshayathiyahya haca aniyana naiy tarsatiy Thatiy Darayava(h)ush khshayathiya mana Auramazda upastam baratuv hada vithibish bagaibish uta imam dahyaum Auramazda patuv haca hainaya haca dushiyara haca drauga aniya imam dahyaum ma.. ajamiya ma haina ma dushiyaram ma drauga aita adam yan - - m jadiyamiy Auramazdam hada ¹vithibish bagaibish aitamaiy Auramazda dadatuv hada vithibish bagaibish.

I.
ANOTHER INSCRIPTION ABOVE THE WALL.

Adam Darayava(h)ush khshayathiya vazraka khshayathiya khshayathiyanam khshayathiya dahyunam tyaisham parunam Vishtaspahya putra Hakhamanishiya Thatiy Darayava(h)ush khshayathiya vashna Auramazdaha ima dahyava tya adam adarshaiy hada ana Parsa kara tya hacama atarsa(n) mana bajim abara(n) (H)uvaja Mada Babirush Arabaya Athura Mudraya Armina Katapatuka Sparda Yauna tyaiy (h)ushkahya uta tyaiy darayahya uta dahyava tya parauvaiy Asagarta Parthava Zara(n)ka Haraiva Bakhtrish Sugda (H)uvarazamiya Thatagush Harauvatish Hi(n)dush Ga(n)dara Saka Maka Thatiy Darayava(h)ush khshayathiya yadiy avatha maniyahy

---
¹ vithibish bagaibish, 86, c.

'haca aniyana ma tarsam imam Parsam karam padiy yadiy kara Parsa pata ahatiy hya duvaishtam shiyatish akhshata hauvciy Aura nirasatiy abiy imam vitham.

B.
OVER THE PILLARS IN THE PALACE.

Darayava(h)ush khshayathiya vazraka khshayathiya khshayathiyanam khshayathiya dahyunam Vishtapahya putra . Hakhamanishiya hya imam tacaram akunaush.

---

[1] haca aniyana ma tarsam, 77, A; 95, B.

Inscriptions of Naqshi Rustam. (NR)

a.

Baga vazraka Auramazda hya imam bumim ada hya avam asmanam ada hya martiyam ada hya shiyatim ada martiyahya hya Darayava(h)um khshayathiyam akunaush aivam paruvnam khshayathiyam aivam paruvnam framataram Adam Darayava(h)ush khshayathiya vazraka khshayathiya khshayathiyanam khshayathiya dahyunam vispazananam khshayathiya ahyaya bumiya vazakaya duraiy apiy Vishtaspahya putra Hakhamanishiya Parsa Parsahya putra Ariya Ariya citra Thatiy Darayava(h)ush khshayathiya vashna Auramazdaha ima dahyava tya adam agarbayam ¹apataram haca Parsa ²adamsham patiyakhshaiy mana bajim abara(n)t(a) tyasham hacama athahy ava akunava(n) datam tya mana aita adari Mada (H)uvaja Parthava Haraiva Bakhtrish Suguda (H)uvarazamish Zara(n)ka Harauvatish Thatagush Ga(n)dara Hi(n)dush Saka Humavarka Saka Tigrakhauda Babirush Athura Arabaya Mudraya Armina Katapatuka Sparda ³Yauna Saka tyaiy taradaraya Skudra Yauna Takabara Putiya Kushiya Maciya Karka Thatiy Darayava(h)ush khshayathiya Auramazda yatha avaina imam bumim yu - - - - pasavadim mana frabara mam khshayathiyam akunaush adam khshayathiya amiy vashna Auramazdaha adamshim gathva niyashadayam ⁴tyasham adam athaham ava akunava(n)ta yatha mam kama aha yadiyadiy tya ⁵ciya(n)karam ava dahyava tya Darayava(h)ush khshayathiya adaraya patikaram didiy tyaiy mana gathum bara(n)tiy yatha ⁶khshnasahadish adataiy azda bavatiy Parsahya martiyahya duray arshtish paragmata adataiy azda bavatiy Parsa martiya

---
¹ apataram haca Parsa, 78.   ² adamsham patiyakhshaiy, 83, B.
³ Yauna, 86, B, Note 1.   ⁴ tyasham - akunava(n)ta, 60, A.   ⁵ ciya(n)-karam ava dahyava, 86.   ⁶ khshnasahadish, 83, B.

duray haca Parsa hamaram patiyajata Thatiy Darayava(h)ush khshayathiya aita tya kartam ava visam vashna Auramazdaha akunavam Auramazdamaiy upastam abara yata kartam akunavam mam Auramazda patuv haca sar - - - utamaiy vitham uta imam dahyaum 'aita adam Auramazdam jadiyamiy aitamaiy Auramazda dadatuv Martiya hya Auramazdaha framana hauvtaiy gasta ma thadaya pathim tyam rastam ma avarada ma starava.

b.

Baga vazraka Auramazda hya ada - - - - - f - - -
- - m tya va - - - - - ada shiyatim martiyahya - - - -
- - u - - - a aruvastam upariy Darayava(h)um khshayathiyam - - - iyasaya Thatiy Darayava(h)ush khshayathiya vashna Auramazdaha - - - - - kar - - - - - -
iya tya - - - - a - - - - tam - - - - - - - ya - - - daush
- - - - - - - athiy n - - - - - - - sh - - - - - uva - - - ya
- - - - - yim karimish - - - - - vasim tya - - - - - - - -
- - - - r - - - - - - iya - - - im - - - - - riyish - - - - - -
ava - - m - - - - - - m m - - - - - m dar - - - - - -
ush - - - a - - - - - - uvish a - - - - - - - - miy - - - - -
ya - - - - astiy darshama da - - - - ya - - - - - au - - -
- - - - iyahya darshama - - - - - - -

c.

Gaubaruva Patishuvarish Darayavahaush khshayathiyahya sharastibara.

d.

Aspacana Darayavahaush khshayathiyahya isuvam dasyama.

e.

Iyam Maciya.

---

¹ aita adam Auramazdam jadiyamiy, 64.

VI.

THE INSCRIPTIONS OF XERXES.

The Inscriptions of Persepolis.

D.

UPON EACH ONE OF THE FOUR PILLARS OF THE ENTRANCES TO THE PALACE OF XERXES.

Baga vazraka Auramazda hya imam bumim ada hya martiyam ada hya shiyatim ada martiyahya hya Khshayarsham khshayathiyam akunaush aivam parunam framataram Adam Khshayarsha khshayathiya vazraka khshayathiya khshayathiyanam khshayathiya dahyunam paruvzananam khshayathiya ahyaya bumiya vazrakaya duraiy apiy Darayavahaush khshayathiyahya putra Hakhamanishiya Thatiy Khshayarsha khshayathiya vazraka vashna Auramazdaha imam duvarthim visadahyum adam akunavam vasiy aniyashciy naibam kartam 'ana Parsa tya adam akunavam utamaiy tya pita akunaush tyapatiy kartam vainataiy naibam ava visam vashna Auramazdaha akuma Thatiy Khshayarsha khshayathiya mam Auramazda patuv utamaiy khshatram uta tya mana kartam uta tyamaiy pitra kartam avashciy Auramazda patuv.

G.

UPON THE PILLARS ON THE WESTERN SIDE OF THE PALACE.

Khshayarsha khshayathiya vazraka khshayathiya khshayathiyanam Darayavahaush khshayathiyahya putra Hakhamanishiya.

---

[1] ana Parsa, 73.

Ea.
UPON THE WALL BY THE STEPS OF THE PALACE.

Baga vazraka Auramazda hya imam bumim ada hya avam asmanam ada hya martiyam ada hya shiyatim ada martiyahya hya Khshayarsham khshayathiyam akunaush aivam parunam khshayathiyam aivam parunam framataram Adam Khshayarsha khshayathiya vazraka khshayathiya khshayathiyanam khshayathiya dahyunam paruvzananam khshayathiya ahiyaya bumiya vazrakaya duraiy apiy Darayavahaush khshayathiyahya putra Hakhamanishiya Thatiy Khshayarsha khshayathiya vazraka vashna Auramazdaha ima hadish adam akunavam mam Auramazda patuv hada bagaibish utamaiy khshatram uta tyamaiy kartam.

Eb.

Baga vazraka Auramazda hya imam bumim ada hya avam asmanam ada hya martiyam ada hya shiyatim ada martiyahya hya Khshayarsham khshayathiyam akunaush aivam parunam khshayathiyam aivam parunam framataram Adam Khshayarsha khshayathiya vazraka khshayathiya khshayathiyanam khshayathiya dahyunam paruvzananam khshayathiya ahiyaya bumiya vazrakaya duraiy apiy Darayavahaush khshayathiyahya putra Hakhamanishiya Thatiy Khshayarsha khshayathiya vazraka vashna Auramazdaha ima hadish adam akunavam mam Auramazda patuv hada bagaibish utamaiy khshatram uta tyamaiy kartam.

Ca.
UPON THE HIGHEST PILLAR NEAR THE SOUTHERN STEPS.

Baga vazraka Auramazda hya imam bumim ada hya avam asmanam ada hya martiyam ada shiyatim ada martiyahya hya Khshayarsham khshayathiyam-

akunaush aivam parunam khshayathiyam aivam
parunam framataram Adam Khshayarsha khshayathiya vazraka khshayathiya khshayathiyanam khshayathiya dahyunam ¹paruv zananam khshayathiya
ahyaya bumiya vazrakaya duraiy apiy Darayavahaush
khshayathiyahya putra Hakhamanishiya Thatiy
Khshayarsha khshayathiya vazraka vashna Aurahya
Mazdaha ima hadish Darayava(h)ush khshayathiya
akunaush hya mana pita mam Auramazda patuv hada
bagaibish uta tyamaiy kartam uta tyamaiy pitra Darayavahaush khshayathiyahya kartam avashciy Auramazda patuv hada bagaibish.

Cb.

Baga vazraka Auramazda hya imam bumim ada
hya avam asmanam ada hya martiyam ada hya shiyatim ada martiyahya hya Khshayarsham khshayathiyam akunaush aivam parunam khshayathiyam
aivam parunam framataram Adam Khshayarsha
khshayathiya vazraka khshayathiya khshayathiyanam
khshayathiya dahyunam ¹paruv zananam khshayathiya ahyaya bumiya vazrakaya duraiy apiy Darayavahaush khshayathiyahya putra Hakhamanishiya
Thatiy Khshayarsha khshayathiya vazraka vashna
Aurahya Mazdaha ima hadish Darayava(h)ush khshayathiya akunaush hya mana pita mam Auramazda
patuv hada bagaibish uta tyamaiy kartam uta tyamaiy pitra Darayavahaush khshayathiyahya kartam
avashciy Auramazda patuv hada bagaibish.

A.

UPON THE STEPS OF THE PALACE.

Baga vazraka Auramazda hya imam bumim ada
avam asmanam ada hya martiyam ada hya shiyatim
ada martiyahya hya Khshayarsham khshayathiyam

---
¹ paruv zananam, 104, Note.

akunaush aivam parunam khshayathiyam aivam parunam framataram Adam Khshayarsha khshayathiya vazraka khshayathiya khshayathiyanam khshayathiya dahyunam paruvzananam khshayathiya ahiyaya bumiya vazrakaya duraiy apiy Darayavahaush khshayathiyahya putra Hakhamanishiya Thatiy Khshayarsha khshayathiya vazraka tya mana kartam ida uta tyamaiy apataram kartam ava visam vashna Auramazdaha akunavam mam Auramazda patuv hada bagaibish utamaiy khshatram uta tyamaiy kartam.

Inscription of Alvend.
F.

Baga vazraka Auramazda hya mathishta baganam hya imam bumim ada hya avam asmanam ada hya martiyam ada hya shiyatim ada martiyahya hya Khshayarsham khshayathiyam akunaush aivam parunam khshayathiyam aivam parunam framataram Adam Khshayarsha khshayathiya vazraka khshayathiya khshayathiyanam khshayathiya dahyunam paruzananam khshayathiya ahiyaya bumiya vazrakaya duraiy apiy Darayavahaush khshayathiya hya putra Hakhamanishiya.

Inscription of Van.

K.

Baga vazraka Auramazda hya mathista baganam hya imam bumim ada hya avam asmanam ada hya martiyam ada hya shiyatim ada martiyahya hya Khshayarsham khshayathiyam akunaush aivam parunam khshayathiyam aivam parunam framataram Adam Khshayarsha khshayathiya vazraka khshayathiya khshayathiyanam khshayathiya dahyunam ¹paruv zananam khshayathiya ahyaya bumiya vazrakaya duraiy apiy Darayavahaush khshayathiyahya putra Hakhamanishiya Thatiy Khshayarsha khshayathiya Darayava(h)ush khshayathiya hya mana pita hauv vashna Auramazdaha vasiy tya naibam akunaush uta ima stanam hauv niyashtaya ka(n)tanaiy yanaiy dipim naiy nipishtam akunaush pasava adam niyashtayam imam dipim nipishtanaiy (Mam Auramazda patuv hada bagaibish utamaiy khshatram uta tyamaiy kartam).

Qa.

UPON THE VASE OF COUNT CAYLUS.

Khshayarsha khshayathiya vazraka.

---
¹ paruv zananam, 104, Note.

VII.

INSCRIPTIONS OF PERSIAN KINGS

AFTER

XERXES.

ARTAXERXES I.

Inscription at Venice.
Qb.
UPON THE VASE IN THE TREASURY OF ST. MARKS.
Ardakhcashca khshayathiya vazraka.

DARIUS II.

Inscriptions of Persepolis.

L.

ABOVE THE POSTS OF THE WINDOWS IN THE PALACE OF DARIUS HYSTASPES.

Ard*a*stan*a* ath*a*(n)g*a*in*a* Dar*a*y*a*v*a*haush khshaya-thiy*a*hya vithiya k*a*rt*a*.

ARTAXERXES MNEMON.*

Inscriptions of Susa. (S.)

a.
UPON THE BASE OF THE PILLARS OF A SMALL ROW OF COLUMNS.

Ad*a*m Artakhsh*a*tra khshay*a*thiya vazr*a*ka khshay*a*thiya khshay*a*thiyanam ¹Dar*a*yava(h)ush*a*hya khshay*a*thiy*a*hya putr*a*.

b.
UPON THE BASE OF THE PILLARS IN THE LARGE ROW OF COLUMNS.

Thatiy Atr*a*khsh*a*tra khshay*a*thiy*a* vazr*a*ka khshay*a*thiya khshay*a*thiyanam khshay*a*thiya d*a*hyunam khshay*a*thiya ahyaya bumiya Dar*a*yava(h)ush*a*hya

---

¹ Dar*a*yava(h)ush*a*hya, 85, A; 24.

* An ingenious attempt to make syntax out of the loose construction shown in these inscriptions of Artaxerxes Mnemon and Artaxerxes Ochus, is the following:
Dar*a*yav*a*(h)ush Vishtasp*a*hya nam*a* putr*a* "D. sohn eines mit namen V." Das folgende jedoch Vishtasp*a*hya Arshama nam*a* putr*a* zeigt wie die vorhergehende genealogische aufzählung eine anakoluthe verbindung zweier nominative, von denen der eine zum andern im genetivverhältnis steht. So merkwürdig das anakoluth in P) ist, so wird es doch durch ein analogon gestützt: es entspricht genau der construction Sz b) h*a*ca Pirav*a* nam*a* raut*a*. In beiden fällen ist statt eines obliquen casus der nominativ gesetzt in folge einer art verkürzung einer bei den alten Persern häufigen pleonastischen ausdruckweise: wie b*a*ca — Pirav*a* nam*a* raut*a* vollständig lauten müsste h*a*ca raut*a* — Pirav*a* nam*a* raut*a* — haca ada, ebenso an unserer stelle m*a*rtiy*a*hya — Arshama nama m*a*rtiya — av*a*hya putr*a*. Eine solche lose anreihung zweier in abhängigkeitsverhältnis zu denkender glieder ist etwas ganz gewöhnliches, z. b. Nisaya nama d*a*hy*a*ush — av*a*d*a*shim avaj*a*n*a*m (Bh. I), (V*a*umis*a*) nama Pars*a* b*a*(n)d*a*k*a* avam ad*a*m fr*a*ish*a*yam (II). Diese constructionen unterscheiden sich von der unsrigen nur dadurch, dass die wiederaufnahme des abhängigen satzgliedes durch eine oblique pronominalform sowohl Sz b) wie an unserer stelle nicht stattgefunden hat. Es ist eine jedermann verständliche vereinfachung jener umständlichen und schwerfälligen ausdrucksweise.

In P) ist auch das wort nam*a*, welches ursprünglich die bedingung der anakoluthen construction ist, als entbehrlich über bord geworfen: Art*a*khsh*a*tra Dar*a*y*a*va(h)ush khshay*a*thiya putr*a* ist also die

khshay*a*thiy*a*hya putr*a* Dar*a*yav*a*(h)ush*a*hya Art*a*khsh*a*trahya khshay*a*thiy*a*hya putr*a* Art*a*khsh*a*trahya Khsh*a*yarsh*a*hya khshay*a*thiy*a*hya putr*a* Khsh*a*yarsh*a*hya Dar*a*yav*a*(h)ush*a*hya khshay*a*thiy*a*hya putr*a* Dar*a*yav*a*(h)ush*a*hya Visht*a*shp*a*hya putr*a* H*a*kham*a*nishiy*a* ¹Im*a*m ap*á*dan*a* Dar*a*yav*a*(h)ush ap*a*nyak*a*m*a* ²akun*a*sh abiy*a*par*a*....pa Art*a*khsh*a*tra nyak*a*m*a*... An*a*hat*a* uta Mithr*a* v*a*shna Aur*a*m*a*zdah*a* ap*a*dana ad*a*m akun*a*v*a*m Aur*a*m*a*zda An*a*hat*a* uta Mithr*a* mam patuv ...

---

weiterentwicklung und vereinfachung des älteren typus Art*a*khsh*a*tra khshay*a*thiy*a*hya — Dar*a*yav*a*(h)ush nam*a* khshay*a*thiy*a* — av*a*hya putr*a* "A. sohn eines königs — es ist ein könig Darius mit namen — dessen sohn."
Noch eine andere eigenheit enthält die inschrift, nämlich den genetiv Vishtap*a*hya, wo wir einen nominativ erwarten. Dieselbe construction findet sich durchgängig in S. Die wiederholung des namens im genetiv statt im nominativ dient zu emphatischer hervorhebung und ist eine assimilatorische anlehnung an den vorbergehenden genetiv, während das subjekt aus dem genetiv zu ergänzen ist: Dar*a*yav*a*(h)ush*a*hya khshay*a*thiy*a*hya putr*a*, Dar*a*v*a*y*a*(h)ush*a*hya (hy*a*) Art*a*khsh*a*tr*a*hya putr*a* "des Darius sohn, (jenes) Darius, (der) des Artaxerxes sohn (war), jenes Artaxerxes, der des Xerxes sohn war u. s. w.—

¹ Im*a*m ap*a*dad*a*, 85, B. ²akun*a*sh, 42.

ARTAXERXES OCHUS.

Inscription of Persepolis.

P.

UPON THE STEPS OF THE PALACE OF DARIUS HYSTASPES AND ARTAXERXES OCHUS.

Baga vazraka Auramazda hya imam bumam ada hya avam asmanam ada hya martiyam ada hya shayatam ada martihya hya mam Artakhshatra khshayathiya akunaush aivam paruvnam khshayathiyam aivam paruvnam framataram Thatiy Artakhshatra khshayathiya vazraka khshayathiya khshayathiyanam khshayathiya dahyunam khshayathiya ahyaya bumiya Adam Artakhshatra khshayathiya putra Artakhshatra Darayava(h)ush khshayathiya putra Artakhshatra khshayathiya putra Artakhshatra Khshayarsha khshayathiya putra Khshayarsha Darayava(h)ush V(i)shtaspahya nama putra V(i)shtaspahya Arshama nama putra Hakhamanishiya Thatiy Artakhshatra khshayathiya imam usatashanam *atha(n)ganam mam upa mam karta Thatiy Artakhshatra khshayathiya mam Auramazda uta M(i)thra baga patuv uta imam dahyum uta ³tya mam karta.

---
¹ Darayava(h)ush, 85, C. ² atha(n)g·nam, 85, D; 86, D. ³ tya mam karta, 85, E and F.

ARSACES.
R.
INSCRIPTION UPON THE SEAL OF GROTEFEND.

Arsh*a*k*a* nam*a* Athiyad*a*ush*a*n*a*hya putr*a*.

THE

CUNEIFORM TEXT*

OF THE

INSCRIPTIONS OF DARIUS

AT

ALVEND, SUEZ, PERSEPOLIS

AND

NAQSHI RUSTAM.

---

* The inscriptions are taken from a pen sketch made by the author.

For the Cuneiform text of the Behistan the student is referred to the great work of Rawlinson in Vol. X of the Royal Asiatic Society of Great Britain and Ireland. The author is under much obligation to Dr. Kossowicz, Professor of Sanskrit in the Imperial University of St. Petersburg.

THE TOMB OF DARIUS.

The Cuneiform Alphabet.

{ Guttural 𒀀 Ā
  Palatal 𒐊 I
  Labial 𒌋 U }   Sonant Sibilant ⟜⟞ z

{ Guttural ⟜ K (𒐊 before U) ≪𒐊 KH ⟨𒐊⟩ G (⟨𒌋⟩ before U)
  Palatal 𒐊⟩ C   ⟜⟨ J (⟜⟨ before U)
  Dental ⟜𒐲 T (𒐲⟩ before U) 𒐊𒐊 TH 𒐊 D (⟨𒐊⟩ before U, ⟜𒐊 before I)
  ⟜⟨ N (≪⟜ before U)
  Labial 𒐊 P.   𒐊⟨ F ⟜𒐊 B ⟜𒐲 M (⟜⟜ before U, ⟜⟨ before I) }

{ Palatal ⟜⟨ Y.
  Lingual ⟜𒐊 R (⟜≪ before U)   Aspiration ⟨⟜⟨
  Labial ⟜𒐊 V (𒐊 before I) }

Sibilants { Lingual ≪ SH
            Dental ⟜⟜ S }

⟜⟨⟜-KHSHĀYATHIYA, ≪≪-BUMI, ⟜𒐊-DAH, 𒐊=TRA.

Numerals

𒐕 1   𒐖𒐕 3   ⟨ 10   ⟨𒐕 12   ⟨⟨ 20
𒐖 2   𒐗 4   ⟨𒐕 11   ⟨𒐖𒐕 13   ⟨⟨𒐕 21
etc.   etc.

A WEDGE SLOPING OBLIQUELY SEPARATES EACH WORD.

(O)

1. 𐎲𐎥 𐏐 𐎺𐏀𐎼𐎣 𐏐 𐎠𐎢𐎼𐎶𐏀𐎭𐎠 𐏐 𐏃𐎹 𐏐 𐎡𐎶𐎠𐎶 𐏐 𐎲𐎢𐎷𐎡𐎶 𐏐 𐎠𐎭𐎠 𐏐 𐏃𐎹 𐏐 𐎠𐎺𐎶 𐏐 𐎠𐎿𐎶𐎠𐎴𐎶 𐏐 𐎠𐎭𐎠 𐏐 𐏃𐎹 𐏐 𐎶𐎼𐎫𐎡𐎹𐎶 𐏐 𐎠𐎭𐎠 𐏐 𐏃𐎹 𐏐 𐏁𐎡𐎹𐎠𐎫𐎡𐎶 𐏐 𐎠𐎭𐎠 𐏐 𐎶𐎼𐎫𐎡𐎹𐏃𐎹𐎠 𐏐 𐏃𐎹 𐏐 𐎭𐎠𐎼𐎹𐎺𐎢𐎶 𐏐 𐎧𐏁𐎠𐎹𐎰𐎡𐎹𐎶 𐏐 𐎠𐎤𐎢𐎴𐎢𐏁 𐏐 𐎠𐎡𐎺𐎶 𐏐 𐎱𐎽𐎢𐎴𐎠𐎶 𐏐 𐎧𐏁𐎠𐎹𐎰𐎡𐎹𐎶 𐏐 𐎠𐎡𐎺𐎶 𐏐 𐎱𐎽𐎢𐎴𐎠𐎶 𐏐 𐎳𐎼𐎶𐎠𐎫𐎠𐎼𐎶 𐏐.

2. 𐎠𐎭𐎶 𐏐 𐎭𐎠𐎼𐎹𐎺𐎢𐏁 𐏐 𐎧𐏁𐎠𐎹𐎰𐎡𐎹 𐏐 𐎺𐏀𐎼𐎣 𐏐 𐎧𐏁𐎠𐎹𐎰𐎡𐎹 𐏐 𐎧𐏁𐎠𐎹𐎰𐎡𐎹𐎠𐎴𐎠𐎶 𐏐 𐎧𐏁𐎠𐎹𐎰𐎡𐎹 𐏐 𐎭𐏃𐎹𐎢𐎴𐎠𐎶 𐏐 𐎱𐎽𐏀𐎴𐎠𐎴𐎠𐎶 𐏐 𐎧𐏁𐎠𐎹𐎰𐎡𐎹 𐏐 𐎠𐏃𐎹𐎠𐎹𐎠 𐏐 𐎲𐎢𐎷𐎡𐎹𐎠 𐏐 𐎺𐏀𐎼𐎣𐎠𐎹𐎠 𐏐 𐎯𐎢𐎼𐎡𐎹 𐏐 𐎠𐎱𐎡𐎹 𐏐 𐎻𐏁𐎫𐎠𐎿𐎱𐏃𐎹𐎠 𐏐 𐎱𐎢𐏂 𐏐 𐏃𐎧𐎠𐎶𐎴𐎡𐏁𐎡𐎹 𐏐.

(SZ)

(London)

(H)

1.

2.

3.

(I)

1.

2.

(I)

1. [cuneiform text]

2. [cuneiform text]

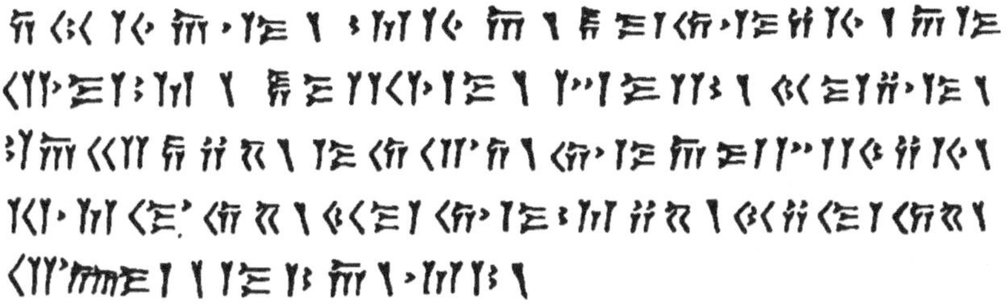

3.

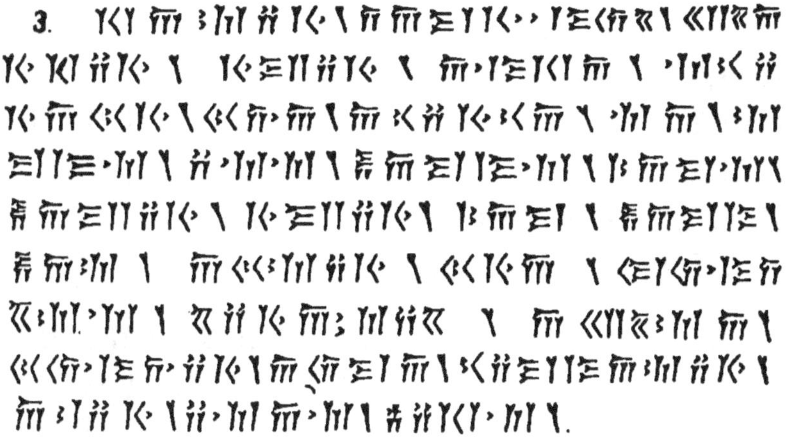

(B)

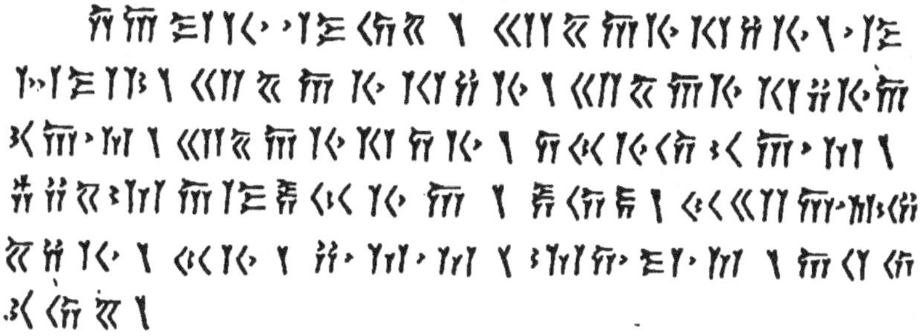

(NR)

a

1. [Old Persian cuneiform text]

2. [Old Persian cuneiform text]

3. [Old Persian cuneiform text]

TRANSLATION

OF THE

INSCRIPTIONS.

THE "SEPULCHRAL' INSCRIPTION OF CYRUS. (M.)

(PERSIAN, MEDIAN, ASSYRIAN.)

The oldest inscription of Persia is found on that structure generally believed to be the tomb of Cyrus. At Pasargadæ, in the midst of the plain of Murghab, stands a building of white marble rising to the height of thirty-six feet from the ground. Its base is forty-seven feet long and forty-four feet broad. A figure in bas-relief carved on a pillar, perhaps the portrait of the king himself, strengthens the theory that this structure is the tomb of Cyrus. A narrow doorway leads into an inner chamber, where Arrian says, the body of Cyrus was placed. Under the relief is the cuneiform inscription, the translation of which follows:

TRANSLATION.

I (am) Cyrus, the king, the Achæmenide.

For the sake of comparison the reader is referred to the epitaph of Cyrus quoted by Strabo, (XV, 3.)

THE INSCRIPTION OF DARIUS HYSTASPES AT BEHISTAN.* (BII.)

(PERSIAN, [MEDIAN, ASSYRIAN.])

1. I (am) Darius, the great king, the king of kings, the king of Persia, the king of countries, the son of Hystaspes, the grandson Arshama, the Achæmenide.

2. Says Darius the king my father (is) Hystaspes, the father of Hystaspes (is) Arshama, the father of Arshama (is) Ariyaramna, the father of Ariyaramna (is Caispis), the father of Caispis (is) Achæmenes.

3. Says Darius the king therefore we are called the Achæmenides: from long ago we have extended† from long ago our family have been kings.

4. Says Darius the king VIII.‡ of my family (there were) who were formerly kings: I am the IX: individually we were (lit. are) kings.

5. Says Darius the king by the grace of Auramazda I am king: Auramazda gave me the kingdom.

6. Says Darius the king these are the countries which came to me: by the grace of Auramazda I became king of them, Persia, Susiana, Babylon, Assyria, Arabia, Egypt, which are by the sea, Sparda, Ionia, Media, Armenia, Cappadocia, Parthia, Drangiana, Area, Chorasmia, Bactriana, Sogdiana, Gandara, Saka, Thatagus, Haravatis, Maka, in all (there are) XXIII countries.

---

*This inscription contains nearly one thousand lines. Cf. Introduction.

†The Persian word AMATA is connected with the Sanskrit root MA *to measure* (Cf. Zend MA and Latin ME-TO). The A is doubtless a prefix corresponding to the Sanskrit A (hither). AMATA would mean *measured hither* or *to the present time*, i. e., reaching to the present. It is possible to emphasize the idea of the root MA (measure): hence the word might signify *measured, tested, tried*.

‡The numerals are represented by horizontal wedges for units and oblique for the tens. Cf. Cuneiform alphabet

7. Says Darius the king these (are) the countries which came to me: by the grace of Auramazda they became subject to me: they bore tribute to me: what was commanded to them by me this was done night and (lit. or) day.

8. Says Darius the king within these countries what man was a friend* him well supported I supported: who was an enemy him well punished I punished; by the grace of Auramazda these countries followed my law: as it was commanded by me to them, so it was done.

9. Says Darius the king Auramazda gave me the kingdom: Auramazda bore me aid until this kingdom was established: by the grace of Auramazda I hold this kingdom.

10. Says Darius the king this (is) what (was) done by me after that I became king; Cambyses by name, the son of Cyrus (was) of our family: he before was king here: of this Cambyses there was a brother Bardiya (i. e., Smerdis) by name possessing a common mother and the same father with Cambyses; afterwards Cambyses slew that Bardiya: when Cambyses slew Bardiya there was not knowledge† (on the part) of the state that Bardiya was slain: afterwards Cambyses went to Egypt: when Cambyses went to Egypt, after that the state became hostile, after that there was deceit to a great extent in the provinces, both Persia and Media and other provinces.

11. Says Darius the king afterwards there was one man, a Magian, Gaumata by name; he rose up from Paishiyauvada; there (is) a mountain Arakadris, by

---

* The Persian word is of doubtful interpretation. It looks like the NOMEN AGENTIS of GAM *to go, a goer hither* or *a comer*. The translation *friend* is a conventional one.

† AZDA, a doubtful word. I connect it with the root DA *to know* which occurs in the compound AURAMAZDA.

name; from there on the 14th day* of the month Viyakhna then it was when he rose up: he then deceived the state; I am Bardiya the son of Cyrus brother of Cambyses: afterwards the whole state became estranged from Cambyses (and) went over to him, both Persia and Media and the other provinces: he seized the kingdom; on the 9th day of the month Garmapada then it was he thus seized the kingdom; afterward Cambyses died by a self-imposed death.†

12. Says Darius the king this kingdom which Gaumata the Magian took from Cambyses, this kingdom from long ago was (the possession) of our family: afterwards Gaumata the Magian took from Cambyses both Persia and Media and the other provinces; he acted in accordance with? his own power? he became king.

13. Says Darius the king there was not a man neither a Persian nor Median nor any one of our family who could make Gaumata the Magian deprived of the kingdom; the state feared him vehemently (or because of his violence); he would smite the state utterly which knew the former Bardiya; for this reason he would smite the state that it might not know me‡ that I am not Bardiya the son of Cyrus; any one did not dare to say anything against Gaumata the Magian until I came; afterwards I asked Auramazda for help; Auramazda bore me aid; on the 10th day of the month Bagayadis then it was I thus with (my) faithful? men slew that Gaumata the Magian and

---

*Lit. with fourteen days; a use of the instrumental which denotes the association of time with an event. This idiom is employed in all like temporal expressions. Cf. Grammar, 72.

†The word uvamarshiyush can be divided into uva *self* (Cf. Skt. sva Lat. se) and marshiyush *die* (Cf. Skt. mar Lat. morior). The meaning also corresponds to the statement in Herodotus III 64-65, that Cambyses died from a wound inflicted by his sword as he was leaping from his horse.

‡Note the direct form of expression.

what men were his foremost allies; there (is) a stronghold Sikayauvatis by name;* there is a province in Media Visaya by name; here I smote him; I took the kingdom from him; by the grace of Auramazda I became king: Auramazda gave me the kingdom.

14. Says Darius the king—the kingdom which was taken away from our family, this I put in (its) place; I established it on (its) foundation; as (it was) formerly so I made it; the sanctuaries? which Gaumata the Magian destroyed I restored. The commerce? of the state and the cattle and the dwelling places, and (I did this) in accordance with† the clans, which Gaumata the Magian took from them, (I restored); I established the state on (its) foundation both Persia and Media and the other provinces; as (it was) formerly so I brought back what (had been) taken away; by the grace of Auramazda this I did; I labored that our clan I might establish in (its) place; as (it was) formerly, so (I made it); I labored by the grace of Auramazda that Gaumata the Magian might not take away our race.

15. Says Darius the king this (is) what I did, after that I became king.

16. Says Darius the king when I slew Gaumata the Magian afterwards there (was) one man Atrina by name the son of Upadara(n)ma; he rose up in Uvaja; (i. e., Susiana); thus he said to the state; I am king in Uvaja; afterwards the people of Uvaja became rebellious (and) went over to that Atrina; he became king in Uvaja; also there (was) one man a Babylonian Naditabira by name the son of Ain....; he rose up in Babylon; thus he deceived the state; I am Na-

---
*Nama is not the accusative of specification, but is attracted into the case, and even the gender of the subject. Lit. there is a stronghold (its) name (is) Sikayauvatis. Cf. Grammar, 61, A. Note 2, but cf. Bartholomæ, Arische Forsch. I, 58.

†Cf. Grammar, 70, A.

bukudracara the son of Nabunita; afterwards the whole of the Babylonian state went over to that Naditabira; Babylon became rebellious; the kingdom in Babylon he seized.

17. Says Darius the king afterwards I sent forth (my army) to Uvaja; this Atrina was led to me bound; I slew him.

18. Says Darius the king afterwards I went to Babylon against that Naditabira who called himself Nabukudracara; the army of Naditabira held the Tigris; there he halted and was on shipboard; afterwards I destroyed the army......one (army) I made submissive, of the other......I led; Auramazda bore me aid; by the grace of Auramazda we crossed the Tigris; here the army of Naditabira I slew utterly; on the 27th day of the month Atriyadiya then it was we thus engaged in battle.

19. Says Darius the king afterwards I went to Babylon; when to Babylon.....................; there (is) a town Zazana by name along the Euphrates; there this Naditabira who called himself Nabukudracara went with his army against me to engage in battle; afterwards we engaged in battle; Auramazda bore me aid; by the grace of Auramazda the army of Naditabira I slew utterly..................... the water bore it away; on the 2nd day of the month Anamaka then it was we thus engaged in battle.

II.

1. Says Darius the king afterwards Naditabira with (his) faithful? horsemen went to Babylon; afterwards I went to Babylon; by the grace of Auramazda I both seized Babylon and seized that Naditabira; afterwards I slew that Naditabira at Babylon.

2. Says Darius the king while I was in Babylon these (are) the provinces which became estranged from me, Persia, Uvaja, Media, Assyria, Armenia, Parthia, Magus, Thatagus, Saka.

3. Says Darius the king there (was) one man Martiya by name, the son of Cicikhris—there (is) a town in Persia Kuganaka by name — here he halted; he rose up in Uvaja; thus he said to the state; I am Imanis king in Uvaja.

4. Says Darius the king then* I was near by Uvaja; afterwards from me .... the people of Uvaja seized that Martiya who was chief of them and slew him.

---

*Old Persian ADa .iy. For various theories respecting the meaning and derivation of AD·ikaiy, cf. F. Müller (Wiener Zeitschrift fur d. k. des Morgenlandes iii), 150, Bartholomæ (Bezz. Beiter X. 272). The theory contained in a late number of the Zeitschr. f. vergl. Sprchfg. is especially deserving of mention. The first element of the compound is ADa (Cf. Skt. ADHa, Lat. inde, Gr. $\H{\epsilon}\nu\theta\alpha$) and the second contains the stem of the interrogative pronoun, ka, (Cf. Skt. ca, Lat. que, Gr. $\tau\varepsilon$). Cf. Lat. tun-c. ,,Den indefiniten und enclitischen gebrauch des fragestamms finden wir abgezogen von andern sprachen (z. b. gr. $\pi o\acute{\iota}$, $\pi\eta$) auch im apers. ciy (*qid), welches einerseits den interrogativstamm selbst indefinit macht (kashsciy), andererseits adverb eine indefinite nebenbedeutung verleiht (paruvamciy ,,früher"). Genau wie das eben angeführte paruvamciy ist unser adakaiy gebildet: das dem -ciy entsprechende kaiy hat nur eine andere casusform. Deren locativische function ist bewahrt (,,in einem gewissen punkte"), hat aber in verbindung mit der zeitpartikel eine temporale bedeutungsmodification erhalten. ada-kaiy bedeutet demnach ,,da zu einer gewissen zeit" ,,da einmal" d. i. ,,damals." Die deutsche partikel ,'damals" und adakaiy stimmen also nicht nur in der bedeutung, sondern auch in der bildungsweise und bedeutungsentwicklung vollkommen überein."

5. Says Darius the king one man Fravartis by name, a Mede, he rose up in Media; thus he said to the state; I am Khshathrita of the family of Uvakhshatara; afterwards the Median state which was in clans became estranged from me (and) went over to that Fravartis; he became king in Media.

6. Says Darius the king the Persian and Median army, which was by him, it was faithful? (lit. a faithful (?) thing); afterwards I sent forth an army; Vidarna* by name, a Persian, my subject him I made chief of them; thus I said to them; go smite that Median army which does not call itself mine; afterwards this Vidarna with the army went away; when he came to Media ...... there (is) a town in Media ...... by name — here he engaged in battle with the Medes; he who was chief among the Medes did not then hold (the army) faithful?; Auramazda bore me aid; by the grace of Auramazda the army of Vidarna smote that rebellious army utterly; on the 6th day of the month Anamaka then it was the battle (was) thus fought by them; afterwards my army — there (is) a region Ka(m)pada by name — there awaited me until I went to Media.

7. Says Darius the king afterwards Dadarsis by name, an Armenian, my subject, him I sent forth to Armenia; thus I said to him; go, the rebellious army which does not call itself mine smite it; afterwards Dadarsis went away; when he came to Armenia, afterwards the rebellious ones having come together went against Dadarsis to engage in battle .... a village ...... by name in Armenia; here they engaged in battle; Auramazda bore me aid; by the grace of Auramazda my army smote that rebellious army utterly; on the 6th day of the month Thuravahara then it was thus the battle (was) fought by them.

---

*Cf Grammar, 61, A, and note 1.

8. Says Darius the king a second time the rebellious ones having come together went against Dadarsis to engage in battle; there (is) a stronghold, Tigra by name, in Armenia — here they engaged in battle; Auramazda bore me aid; by the grace of Auramazda, my army smote that rebellious army utterly; on the 18th day of the month, Thuravahara then it was the battle (was) thus fought by them.

9. Says Darius the king a third time the rebellious ones having come together went against Dadarsis to engage in battle; there (is) a stronghold, U....ama by name, in Armenia — here they engaged in battle; Auramazda bore me aid; by the grace of Auramazda my army smote that rebellious army utterly; on the 9th day of the month, Thaigarcis then it was thus the battle (was) fought by them; afterwards Dadarsis awaited me until I came to Media.

10. Says Darius the king afterwards Vaumisa by name, a Persian, my subject, him I sent forth to Armenia; thus I said to him; go, the rebellious army which does not call itself mine, smite it; afterwards Vaumisa went away; when he came to Armenia afterwards, the rebellious ones having come together went against Vaumisa to engage in battle; there (is) a region, ... by name, in Assyria—here they engaged in battle; Auramazda bore me aid; by the aid of Auramazda my army smote that rebellious army utterly; on the 15th day of the month Anamaka, then it was thus the battle (was) fought by them.

11. Says Darius the king a second time the rebellious ones having come together went against Vaumisa to engage in battle; there (is) a region Autiyara by name in Armenia—here they engaged in battle; Auramazda bore me aid; by the grace of Auramazda my army smote that rebellious army utterly; .... of the month Thuravahara ...... thus the battle

(was) fought by them; afterwards Vaumisa awaited me in Armenia until I came to Media.

12. Says Darius the king afterwards I went from Babylon; I went away to Media; when I went to Media—there (is) a town Kudurus by name in Media —here this Fravartis (i. e., Phaortes)' who called himself king in Media went with (his) army against me to engage in battle; afterwards we engaged in battle; Auramazda bore me aid; by the grace of Auramazda I smote the army of Fravartis utterly; on the 26th day of the month Adukanis then it was we engaged in battle.

13. Says Darius the king afterwards this Fravartis with faithful ? horsemen—in that place (was) a region Raga by name in Media—here went; afterwards I sent forth my army against them; Fravartis was seized (and) led to me; I cut off (his) nose and ears and tongue, and to him .... I led; he was held bound at my court; the whole state saw him; afterwards I put (him) on a cross at Ecbatana, and what men were his foremost allies, these I threw within a prison at Ecbatana.

14. Says Darius the king one man, Citra(n)takhma by name, a Sagartian, he became rebellious to me; thus he said to the state; I am king in Sagartia, of the family of Uvakhshatara; afterwards I sent forth the Persian and Median army; Takhmaspada by name, a Mede, my subject, him I made chief of them; thus I said to them; go, the rebellious army, which does not call itself mine, smite it; afterwards Takhmaspada went away with the army (and) engaged in battle with Citra(n)takhma; Auramazda bore me aid; by the grace of Auramazda my army smote that rebellious army utterly and seized Citra(n)takhma (and) brought (him) to me; afterwards I cut off his nose and ears, and to him ..... I led; he was held bound at my

court; the whole state saw him; afterwards I put him on a cross in Arabia.

15. Says Darius the king this (is) what (was) done by me in Media.

16. Says Darius the king Parthia and Hyrcania .... of Fravartis .... called himself; Hystaspes my father .... army .... afterwards Hystaspes ... allies .... town ... by name ...... they engaged in battle .... thus the battle (was) fought by them.

III.

1. Says Darius the king afterwards I sent forth the Persian army to Hystaspes from Raga; when this army came to Hystaspes, afterwards Hystaspes with that army went away—there (is) a town Patigrabana by name in Parthia—here he engaged in battle with the rebellious ones; Auramazda bore me aid; by the grace of Auramazda Hystaspes smote that rebellious army utterly; on the first day of the month Garmapada then it was that thus the battle (was) fought by them.

2. Says Darius the king afterwards it became my province; this (is) what (was) done by me in Parthia.

3. Says Darius the king there (is) a region Margus by name; it became rebellious to me; one man Frada, a Margianian, him they made chief; afterwards I sent forth Dadarsis by name, a Persian, my subject, satrap in Bactria against him; thus I said to him: go, smite that army which does not call itself mine; afterwards Dadarsis with the army went away (and) engaged in battle with the Margianians; Auramazda bore me aid; by the grace of Auramazda my army smote that rebellious army utterly; on the 23rd day of the month Atriyadiya then it was thus the battle (was) fought by them.

4. Says Darius the king afterwards it became my province; this (is) what (was) done by me in Bactria.

5. Says Darius the king one man Vahyazdata by name—there (is) a town Tarava by name; there (is) a region Yutiya by name in Persia—here halted; he a second time (i. e., after Gaumata) rose up in Persia; thus he said to the state; I am Bardiya the son of Cyrus; afterwards the Persian army which (was) in clans departed from duty; it became estranged from me (and) went over to that Vahyazdata; he became king in Persia.

6. Says Darius the king afterwards I sent forth the

Persian and Median army which was by me; Artavardiya by name, a Persian, my subject, him I made chief of them; the other Persian army went with (lit. after) me to Media; afterwards Artavardiya with the army went to Persia; when he came to Persia—there (is) a town Rakha by name in Persia—here this Vahyazdata who called himself Bardiya went with (his) army against Artavardiya to engage in battle; afterwards they engaged in battle; Auramazda bore me aid; by the grace of Auramazda my army smote that army of Vahyazdata utterly; on the 12th day of the month Thuravahara then it was thus the battle (was) fought by them.

7. Says Darius the king afterwards this Vahyazdata with faithful? horsemen then went to Paishiyauvada; from thence he went with an army again against Artavardiya to engage in battle; there (is) a mountain Paraga by name—here they engaged in battle; Auramazda gave me aid; by the grace of Auramazda my army smote that army of Vahyazdata utterly; on the 6th day of the month Garmapada then it was thus the battle (was) fought by them and they seized that Vahyazdata and what men were his foremost allies, they seized.

8. Says Darius the king afterwards—there (is) a a town is Persia Uvadaidaya by name*—here, that Vahyazdata and what men were his foremost allies, them I put on a cross.

9. Says Darius the king this Vahyazdata who called himself Bardiya he sent forth an army to Harauvatis —there (was) Vivana by name, a Persian, my subject, satrap in Harauvatis—against him (he sent an army)

---

*The reader has noticed the constant use of paratax. Instead of bringing the words of the sentence into syntax independent constructions are employed. In no other language is this loose arrangement (which we must feel was original to speech) shown to better advantage than in the old Persian inscriptions. Cf. Grammar, 59.

and one man he made chief of them; thus he said to them: go, smite that Vivana and that army which calls itself of Darius the king, afterwards this army, which Vahyazadata sent forth, went against Vivana, to engage in battle; there is a stronghold Kapishakanis by name—here they engaged in battle; Auramazda bore me aid; by the grace of Auramazda my army smote that rebellious army utterly; on the 13th day of the month Anamaka then it was thus the battle (was) fought by them.

10. Says Darius the king again the rebellious ones having come together went against Vivana to engage in battle; there (is) a region Ga(n)dutava by name—here they engaged in battle; Auramazda bore me aid; by the grace of Auramazda my army smote that rebellious army utterly; on the 8th day of the month Viyakhna then it was thus the battle (was) fought by them.

11. Says Darius the king afterwards this man, who was chief of that army which Vahyazdata sent against Vivana, this chief with faithful ? horseman went away —there (is) a stronghold Arshada by name in Harauvatis—he went beyond thence; afterwards Vivana, with an army on foot went (against) them; here he seized him and what men were his foremost allies he slew.

12. Says Darius the king afterwards the province became mine; this is what was done by me at Harauvatis.

13. Says Darius the king when I was in Persia and Media a second time the Babylonians became estranged from me; one man, Arakha by name, an Armenian son of Han(?)dita,* he rose up in Babylon;

---

*The N in Handita as well as the N in Dubana conjecture has supplied. The combination of wedges in the cuneiform text resembles no other characters on the stone and perhaps is the sign for L which otherwise would be wanting in the Old Persian alphabet. I, however, feel that it is simply a careless writing of the nasal.

there (is) a region, Duban(?)a by name—from there he rose up; thus he lied; I am Nabukudracara, the son of Nabunita; afterwards the Babylonian state became estranged from me (and) went over to that Arakha; he seized Babylon; he became king in Babylon.

14. Says Darius the king afterwards I sent forth my army to Babylon; Vi(n)dafra by name, a Mede, my subject, him I made chief; thus I said to them; go, smite that army in Babylon which does not call itself mine; afterwards Vi(n)dafra with an army went to Babylon; Auramazda bore me aid; by the grace of Auramazda, Vi(n)dafra seized Babylon............ on the 2d day of the month......then it was thus...
....
....
....

IV.

1. Says Darius the king this (is) what was done by me in Babylon.

2. Says Darius the king this (is) what I did; by the grace of Auramazda it was (done) wholly in (my) way;* after that the kings became rebellious I engaged in XIX battles; by the grace of Auramazda I smote them† and I seized IX kings; there was one, Gaumata by name, a Magian; he lied; thus he said; I am Bardiya the son of Cyrus; he made Persia rebellious; there (was) one, Atrina by name, in Uvaja; he lied; thus he said; I am king in Uvaja; he made Uvaja rebellious to me; there (was) one, Naditabira by name, a Babylonian; he lied; thus he said; I am Nabukudracara the son of Nabunita; he made Babylon rebellious; there (was) one, Martiya by name, a Persian; he lied; thus he said; I am Imanis king in Uvaja; he made Uvaja rebellious; there (was) one Fravartis by name, a Mede; he lied; thus he said; I am Khshathrita of the family of Uvakhshatara; he made Media rebellious; there (was) one, Citra(n)takhma by name, in Sagartia; he lied; thus he said; I am King in Sagartia, of the family of Uvakhshatara; he made Sagartia rebellious; there (was) one, Frada by name, a Margianian; he lied; thus he said; I am a king in Margus, he made Margus rebellious; there (was) one, Vahyazdata by name, a Persian; he lied; thus he said; I am Bardiya the son of Cyrus; he made Persia rebellious; there (was) one, Arakha by name, an Armenian; he lied; thus he said; I am Nabukudracara the son of Nabunita; he made Babylon rebellious.

---

*HAMAHYAYA THARDA is of doubtful interpetation. Rawl suggested "the performance of the whole"; Oppert "dans toute ma vie; dans toute l'annie, toujours"; Spiegel "in aller Weiser." Many attempts have been made to connect THARDA with the Sanskrit ÇARAD, *autumn* used in the Veda metaphorically for *year*. Cf. Grammar, 80, c.

† Or *smote theirs*, i. e., their forces. Cf. Grammar, 83, B.

3. Says Darius the king these IX kings I seized within these battles.

4. Says Darius the king these (are) the provinces which became rebellious; a lie made them*....that these deceived the state; afterwards Auramazda made them in my hand; as desire (moved) me, thus.......

5. Says Darius the king O thou who wilt be king in the future, protect thyself strongly from deceit; whatever man will be a deceiver, him punish well (lit. him well punished punish. Cf., I. 8), if thus thou shalt think "may my country be firm."

6. Says Darius the king this (is) what I did; by the grace of Auramazda I did (it) wholly in (my) way;† O thou who shalt examine this inscription in the future, let it convince thee (as to) what (was) done by me; do not deceive thyself.

7. Says Darius the king Auramazda (is) a witness? that this (is) true (and) not false (which) I did wholly in my way.‡

8. Says Darius the king by the grace of Auramazda .... (what) else (was) done by me to a great extent, that (is) not inscribed on this inscription; for this reason it (is) not inscribed lest whoever will examine this inscription in the future............. it may not convince him (as to) what (was) done by me (and) he may think (it) false.§

9. Says Darius the king who were the former kings, by these nothing (was) done to a great extent as (was)

---

*Perhaps we can supply with Spiegel HAMITRIYA *a lie made them rebellious*.

†Cf. IV. 2.

‡Cf. IV. 2.

§Although much has become obliterated yet we have enough to enable us to gain the sense of the passage. The idea is: should I write the memorial of all my achievements, they would be so many that men would lose faith in the testimony of this stone.

performed* wholly by me through the grace of Auramazda.

10. Says Darius the king.........let it convince thee (as to) what (was) done by me; thus.......... for this reason do not hide (this monument); if thou shalt not hide this monument (but) tell (it) to the state, may Auramazda be a friend to thee and may there be to thee a family abundantly and live thou long.

11. Says Darius the king if thou shalt hide this monument (and) not tell (it) to the state, may Auramazda be a smiter to thee and may there not be to thee a family.

12. Says Darius the king this (is) what I did wholly in (my) way;† by the grace of Auramazda I did (it); Auramazda bore me aid and the other gods which are.

13. Says Darius the king for this reason Auramazda bore me aid and the other gods which are, because I was not an enemy, I was not a deceiver, I was not a despot...............family above law, above me ....I did......that whoever for me helped those belonging to my race, him well supported I supported; whenever.............him well punished I punished.

14. Says Darius the king O thou who art king in the future, whatever man shall be a deceiver........ shall be..........(be) not a friend to these; punish these with severe punishment.

15. Says Darius the king O thou who shalt see this inscription in the future which I inscribed or these pictures, thou shalt not destroy (them)‡ as long as thou shalt live; thus guard them.

---

*Cf. IV. 2, but here THARDA fails to appear.
†Cf. IV. 2.
‡Old Persian YAVA. „Für das auffällige —a scheinen mir und zwei möglichkeiten offen: es konnte yava nach abfall des t als flectierbarer a-stamm vom sprachgefühl aufgefasst an das femininum tauma sich formell anschliessen (mit einbusse der conjunctionalen bedeutung),

16. Says Darius the king if thou shalt see this inscription or these pictures (and) shalt not destroy them and shalt guard them for me as long as (thy) family shall be, may Auramazda be a friend to thee and may there be to thee a family abundantly and live thou long and whatever thou shalt do, this for thee (let) Auramazda......let him grant thy prayers.

19. Says Darius the king if thou shalt see this inscription or these pictures (and) shalt destroy them and shalt not guard them for me as long as (thy) family shall be, may Auramazda be a smiter to thee and may there not be to thee a family and whatever thou shalt do this let Auramazda destroy for thee.

18. Says Darius the king these (are) the men who were there then when I slew Gaumata the Magian who called himself Bardiya; then these men co-operated as my allies; Vi(n)dafrana by name, the son of Vayaspara, a Persian; Utana by name, the son of Thukhra, a Persian; Gauburuva by name, the son of Marduniya, a Persian; Vidarna by name, the son of Magabigna, a Persian; Bagabukhsha by name, the son of Daduhya, a Persian; Ardumanis by name, the son of Vahauka, a Persian.

19. Says Darius the king O thou who art king in the future, what............what Darius............
....
....
........................I did.

---

oder es hat nach analogie von yatha, yata („bis, wärend") und andern auf -a ausleutenden conjunctionen selbst langen auslaut erhalten.
Wehn allerdings Bh. IV, 71 yava ji[vahy] zu lesen ist, so bleibt die zweite erklärung allein übrig. Die gegenseitige beeinflussung von partikeln bietet nichts auffallendes; es kann ἄνευς (Brugmann Griech. Gramm. §200) neben ἄνευ, ngr. ἀντίς neben ἀντί, τότες neben τότε u. ä. nach analogie von μέχρι-ς etc., sowie überhaupt das umsichgreifen des auslautenden -s in griech. partikeln (οὕτω-ς, ὡς, etc.) verglichen werden." (A. T.)
J. Schmidt explains YAVA as neuter plural (172).

V.

1. Says Darius the king this (is) what I did ......
.... way ....
.........king.............province; this became estranged from me; one man ..imina by name; the (people) of Uvaja made him chief; afterwards I seut forth (my) army to Uvaja; one man Gaubaruva by name, a Persian, my subject, him I made chief of them; afterwards this Gaubaruva with an army went to Uvaja; he engaged in battle with the rebellious ones; afterwards ....
.... and to him ....
.... he seized and led to me......................province.............
.... thus it ....
....
2. Says Darius the king ....
....
.... Auramazda .... by the grace of Auramazda................ I did.
3. Says Darius the king whoever in the future ....
....
....
4. Says Darius the King .... I went against Saka..............................
..........Tigris..............to the sea ....
.... I seized the enemy .... to ......
.... Saku(n)ka by name, him I seized ......
.... there another as chief ....
.... afterwards ....
....
5. Says Darius the king .... not Auramazda .... if by the grace of Auramazda .... I did.

6. Says Darius the king ...... worship? Auramazda
....
....
....

Kossowicz remarks: "Notatu dignum, omnium, quantum scio, imperatorum, qui armorum vi atque gloria celebres extiterant, nisi duo, Darium Hystaspi nempe et Napoleonem I — mum, commilitonum nomina; victorias suas recensendo, in publicis monumentis memoriae tradidisse."

The Smaller Inscriptions of Behistan.

a.
OVER THE PICTURE OF DARIUS.*

I (am) Darius, the great king, king of kings, king of Persia, king of the countries, the son of Hystaspes, the grandson of Arshama, the Achaemenide. Says Darius the king my father (is) Hystaspes, the father of Hystaspes (is) Arshama, the father of Arshama (is) Ariyaramna, the father of Ariyaramna (is) Caispis, the father of Caispis (is) Achaemenes. Says Darius the king therefore we are called Achaemenides; from long ago we have extended; from long ago our family have been kings. Says Darius the king VIII of my family (there were) who were formerly kings; I am the ninth IX; individually we are kings.

b.
UNDER THE PROSTRATE FORM.

This Gaumata the Median lied; thus he said; I am Bardiya, the son of Cyrus; I am king.

c.
OVER THE FIRST STANDING FIGURE.

This Atrina lied; thus he said; I am king in Uvaja.

d.
OVER THE SECOND STANDING FIGURE.

This Naditabira lied; thus he said; I am Nabuk(u)dracara, the son of Nabunita; I am king in Babylon.

e.
UPON THE GARMENT OF THE THIRD STANDING FIGURE.

This Fravartis lied; thus he said; I am Khshathrita of the family of Uvakhshatara; I am king in Media.

---
*Cf. I, 1–4.

f.
OVER THE FOURTH STANDING FIGURE.

This Martiya lied; thus he said; I am Imanis, king in Uvaja.

g.
OVER THE FIFTH STANDING FIGURE.

This Citra(n)takhma lied; thus he said; I am king in Sagartia, of the family of Uvakhshatara.

h.
OVER THE SIXTH STANDING FIGURE.

This Vahyazdata lied; thus he said; I am Bardiya, the son of Cyrus; I am king.

i.
OVER THE SEVENTH STANDING FIGURE.

This Arakha lied; thus he said; I am Nabuk(u)dracara, the son of Nabunita; I am king in Babylon.

j.
OVER THE EIGHTH STANDING FIGURE.

This Frada lied; thus he said; I am king in Margus.

k.
OVER THE NINTH STANDING FIGURE.*

This (is) Saku(n)ka, the Sakian.

---

*Herodotus mentions the high cap which was peculiar to the garb of the Sakians. It is interesting to note that the figure is represented on the stone wearing this national head-dress.

The Inscription of Alvend. (O.)

(PERSIAN.)

This inscription is engraven upon two niches on a large block of stone near the base of Mt. Alvend. Not only is the monumental fame of Darius perpetuated by the Behistan mountain, but in different parts of the Persian empire this monarch caused to be inscribed historic records of his reign. At Persepolis the palaces declare the name of their founder and his prayers for the protection of heaven. To Darius beyond all others we are indebted for what we have of the Paleography of Persia.

I TRANSLATION.

A great God (is) Auramazda who created this earth, who created yonder heaven,* who created man, who created the† spirit? of man, who made Darius king, one king of many, one lord of many. I (am) Darius the great king, king of kings, king of the countries possessing many kinds of people, king of this great earth far and wide, the son of Hystaspes, the Achæmenide.

---

*ASMAN (*heaven*) is literally *a stone* as we know from its cognate in Sanskrit. Probably the Persians regarded the sky as a solid dome; cf. the Hebrew word RAQI(A) (Gen. I. 8.) and our *firmament* (firmamentum).

†The old Persian SHIYATIS is the Avest. SHAITI. The Assyrian translates the word by DUMQU "blessing." But cf. Fick, idg. Wb. I² 233, and J. Schmidt Plur. d. idg. Ntr. 418.

The Inscriptions of Suez. (SZ.)
(PERSIAN, MEDIAN, ASSYRIAN, EGYPTIAN.)

A crowned head is carved upon the stone together with the following legend:

TRANSLATION.
A.
Darius the great king; king of kings, king of the countries, the son of Hystaspes, the Achaemenide.

Above are a dozen lines of Persian cuneiform text the translation of which follows:

TRANSLATION.
B.
A great god (is) Auramazda, who created yonder heaven, who created this earth, who created man, who created the spirit*? of man, who made Darius king, who gave the kingdom to Darius; what great
....
I (am) Darius the great king, king of kings, king of the countries possessing many people, king of this great earth far and wide, son of Hystaspes, the Achaemenide. Says Darius the king I am a Persian; with (the help of) Persia I seized Egypt; I commanded to dig this canal,† from the Nile by name a river which flows in Egypt, to the sea which goes from Persia; afterwards this canal was dug there as I commanded....
....
....
....

---
*Cf. note under (O).
†Cf. Herodotus, IV. 39.

The Inscription of London.

(PERSIAN, MEDIAN, ASSYRIAN.)

The following short inscription can be seen in the British Museum on a cylinder which furnishes a fine specimen of gem engraving. A warrior in his chariot is represented as attacking at full speed a lion,* the symbol of power. This warrior from his crown we can interpret as King Darius. He holds his bow ready for action, while the charioteer urges on the steeds. This cylinder was carried to England from Egypt.

TRANSLATION.

I (am) Darius the king.

---

*On the Persian sculptures, the lion and bull occur often, as emblems of strength. Metaphors of this kind are frequent in all oriental literature. In making a list of the epithets of the god Indra in the Veda, one is struck with the repeated comparisons of this sort. However, the Vedic poets drew from the stall as the most fertile source of metaphors, and it was the later Sanskrit which used the beasts of the forest more extensively for that purpose. (e. g., the tiger of men, etc.) In Biblical literature the reader is referred to Ezekiel i. 10. "As for the likeness of their faces, they four had the faces of man, and the face of a lion on the right side." Daniel vii. 4. "The first was like a lion and had eagles' wings." The familiar national emblems of later date, the Roman eagle, the British lion, etc., all had their origin in this early conception.

The Inscriptions of Darius at Persepolis.

(PERSIAN, [MEDIAN, ASSYRIAN.])

The inscriptions of Persepolis show that same spirit of patriotism which characterizes the record on Mt. Behistan. The superiority of Persia over the provinces of the empire is set forth by the monarch with the purpose of elevating the feelings of his countrymen and of keeping alive ever in their hearts the love of country. The palace of Darius shows the ruins of several departments with external chambers which were evidently guard-rooms. The roof of a large room, fifty feet square, was supported by pillars, the bases of which remain to-day. This edifice is one of those ruins which represent the combined work of several successive Achaemenian kings. All the structures stand upon the same platform around which are great walls of hewn stone. Two inscriptions are found above the wall and one on two pillars, which read as follows:

TRANSLATION.

H.

ABOVE THE WALL SURROUNDING THE PALACE.

The great Auramazda, who (is) the greatest of the gods, he made Darius king; he gave to him the kingdom; by the grace of Auramazda Darius (is) king. Says Darius the king this (is) the country Persia which Auramazda gave me, which, beautiful, possessing good horses, possessing good men, by the grace of Auramazda and (by the achievements) of me Darius the king, does not fear an* enemy.(?) Says Darius the king let Auramazda bear me aid with (his) fellow gods and let Auramazda protect this country from an army, from misfortune, from deceit; may not an enemy .... come unto this country, nor an army,

---
*Or, THE OTHER (i. e., AHRIMAN). Cf. note to (I).

nor misfortune nor deceit; this I pray of Auramazda
.... with (his) fellow gods; this let Auramazda give
me with (his) fellow gods.

I.

ANOTHER INSCRIPTION ABOVE THE WALL.

I (am) Darius the great king, king of kings, king
of many countries, the son of Hystaspes, the Achaemenide. Says Darius the king by the grace of
Auramazda these (are) the provinces which I subdued
with (the help of) that Persian army, (and) which
feared me (and) brought to me tribute; Uvaja, Media,
Babylon, Arabia, Assyria, Egypt, Armenia, Cappadocia, Sparda, Ionia, which (are) of the dry (land)
(and) which (are) of the sea, and the provinces which
(are) in the east, Sagartia, Parthia, Zara(n)ka, Haraiva, Bactria, Sugda, Uvarazamiya, Thatagus, Harauvatis, India, Ga(n)dara, Saka, Maka. Says Darius
the king if thus thou shalt think "may I not fear an
enemy,"* protect this Persian state; if the Persian
state shall be protected, may this goddess (namely)
this spirit (of patriotism) for a long time unharmed,
descend upon this race.

B.

OVER THE PILLARS IN THE PALACE.

Darius the great king, king of kings, king of the
countries, the son of Hystapes, the Achaemenide,
who built this palace.

---

* Dr. Julius Oppert understood the Old Persian word ANIYa (other)
to be the only notion of AHRIMAN found in the inscriptions. He ar-
gued that the word ANIYa never means "enemy:" The prayer he
translated "The good Principle, which has always destroyed the
Hater (DUVaISaTaM) will descend on this house."

The Inscription on the Tomb of Darius. (NR.)
(PERSIAN, MEDIAN, ASSYRIAN.)

Naqshi—Rustam is the burial place of Darius.

On the face of a mountain which rises to the perpendicular height of 900 feet are cut the excavations which are doubtless tombs. These relics have a common external appearance. They are carved into the rock fourteen feet deep in the form of a cross, the upright section of which is about ninety feet, the transverse division about fifty feet. Four pilasters about seven feet apart ornament the transverse section, in the midst of which is the door of the tomb. On the division above the façade of this sepulchre are the sculptures. A double row of fourteen figures supports two cornices. Two bulls form the pillars at each end of the upper cornice. On an elevated pedestal of three steps stands a figure dressed in a flowing robe, holding his bow in his left hand. Without doubt this is the effigy of him who lies buried beneath. Opposite the standing form, on a pedestal of three steps, is an altar, upon which the sacred fire is burning, while above is a disk, probably representing the sun, of which the fire blazing at the shrine is the symbol. Above is the image of Auramazda. One of these structures Ker-Porter visited, and with great difficulty explored its interior. Although he was not able to read the inscription, yet he conjectured that this was the tomb of Darius. I quote him at this point. "The second tomb is the only one whereon the marks of an inscription can be traced; but over the whole tablet of the upper compartment letters are visible wherever they could be introduced; above the figures, between them and the altar, along the side, from top to bottom; in short, everywhere we see it covered with the arrow-headed characters and in good preservation. What a treasure of information doubtless is there to the happy man who can decipher it. It was tantalizing to a painful degree to look at such a sealed book in the very spot of mystery, where probably its contents would explain all. But it certainly is a very distinguishing peculiarity of this tomb that it alone should contain any inscription, and that the writing on it is so abundant; a circumstance that might warrant the supposition of this being the tomb that was cut by the express orders of Darius Hystaspes to receive his remains." (Travels in Georgia, Persia, Armenia, ancient Babylonia, etc., etc., by Sir Robert Ker-Porter, vol. I, p. 523.)

Before translating the inscription I wish to call the attention of the reader to Herod. III, 88.

TRANSLATION.

A.

A great god is Auramazda, who created this earth, who created yonder heaven, who created man, who created the spirit* of man, who made Darius king, one king of many, one lord of many. I (am) Darius the great king, king of kings, king of the countries possessing many kinds of people, king of this great earth far and wide, son of Hystaspes the Achaemenide, a Persian, the son of a Persian: an Aryan, an Aryan offspring. Says Darius the king by the grace of Auramazda these (are) the provinces which I seized afart† from Persia; I ruled them; they brought tribute to me .... what was commanded to them by me, this they did; the law which (is) mine that was established; Media, Uvaja, Parthia, Haraiva, Bactria, Suguda, Uvarazamis, Zara(n)ka Harauvatis, Thatagus, Ga(n)dara, India, Sakae, Humavarkae, Sakae Tigrakhaudae, Babylon, Assyria, Arabia, Egypt, Armenia,

---

*Cf. note to (O).

†Or, **except Persia**.

SUPPLEMENTARY NOTE TO NRa.

As this volume goes to press an article (published in 1893) comes from the pen of the distinguished scholar Hübschmann. He insists on "übel" as the signification of GaSTa (NRa) against Thumb's argument (published in 1891) which I have quoted at some length on p. 147. I add a few extracts.

"Auf diese erklärung Kern's greift nun A. Thumb zurück, ohne die gründe, die für Spiegel's deutung sprechen, zu erwägen. Diese gründe aber sind durchaus stichhaltig und werfen Thumb's erklärung um. GaSTa ist in der keilschrift 2. gattung durch ein wort übersetzt, das früher *siyunika*, von Oppert...... *visnika*, von Weisbach...... *mushnika* gelesen wird, dessen bedeutung aber nicht zweifelhaft ist......... und sein aequivalent im Babylonischen text ist *bi-i-shi*, das ,,böse" bedeutet.*

Wie mit GaSTa, steht es auch mit THaDaYa; die alte erklärung† ist die richtige........Meine übersetzung lautete: O mensch, der befehl des Ahuramazda, er soll dir nicht übel erscheinen." ‡

---

*BISHU seems to render into Assyrian the Persian ARIKa (ARaIKa?) "enemy."

†i. e., As an augmentless imperfect third singular (Cf. Grammar 95B.) and connected with Avestan *sad* "seem".

‡Cf. Oppert's translation of the Median "homo quae est Oromazis doctrina, illa tibi mala ne videatur". Also cf. translation of the Median given in foot note on p. 149.

Cappadocia, Sparda, Ionia, Sakae beyond the sea, the Ionians wearing long hair* Patians Kusians, Macians, Karkians. Says Darius the king Auramazda when he saw this earth .... afterwards gave it to me; he made me king; I am king; by the grace of Auramazda I established it on (its) foundation; what I commanded to them, this they did as desire came to (lit. was) me. If perchance thou shalt think that manifold (lit. a manifold thing) are these provinces which Darius the king held, look at the picture (of those) who are bearing my throne,† in order that thou mayest know them; then to thee will be the knowledge (that) the spear of a Persian man hath gone forth afar; then to thee will be the knowledge (that) a Persian man waged battle far from Persia. Says Darius the king this (is) what (was) done; all this by the grace of Auramazda I did; Auramazda bore me aid until this was done, let Auramazda protect me from .... and my race and this country; this I pray of Auramazda; this let Auramazda give me. O man, what (are) the commands of Auramazda, may he (make them) revealed to thee; do not err; do not leave the right path, do not sin.‡

---

*Cf. the Homeric καρηκομώοντες.

†The northern throne of the great palace contains five tiers of ten warriors supporting the platform on which the king is represented sitting, surrounded by his attendants.

‡Cf. Bartholomae Bezz. Beitr. X, 269, and Kern (ZDMG. XXIII, 222). For meaning of. MA STARAVA, cf. Mélanges, Asiat. III, 344. Thumb (Zeitschrift für vgl. Sprachforsch, 1891) translates ,,O menschl lass dir die lehre des Auramazda gesagt sein. Verabscheue sie nicht den richtigen weg (d. h. die lehre des A.), beflecke ihn nicht." I quote an extract,

"Zunächst halte ich die erklärung von gasta als ,,stinkend — widerwärtig" wegen der merkwürdigen bedeutungsübertragung ins ethische für unwahrscheinlich und ziehe die von selbst sich aufdrängende zugehörigkeit zu ai. gad ,,sagen, sprechen" vor. Kern hat dies schon längst gesehen und in dem worte das part. auf -ta erkannt; aber bei einem transitiven verbum durch die annahme medialer bedeutung

B.

A great god (is) Auramazda who ....
...... made spirit? of man ....
above Darius the king ....
.... Says Darius the king
by the grace of Auramazda ....
....
....
.... is violence ....
....
...... violence ....

Jenes verbaladjectivs den activen sinn „(er) hat gesagt" herauszubringen, ist nicht weniger gezwungen. g«sta ist regelmässiges passives particip und muss mit hya zusammenconstruiert werden, welches ich als optativ der copula (*siet) fasse. Es ist daher zu übersetzen: „möge dir gesagt sein die lehre des Auramazda," „lass dir gesagt sein," d. h. „halte fest an ... ". Einen optativ hat in hya schon Bopp (Lautsystem d. apers. p. 149) vermutet, wenn auch seine weitere erklärung eine ganz andere, verfehlte ist. Wir gewinnen durch die von uns vorgeschlagene constructionsweise eine genaue parallele zu J. 22 f. hya duvaistam shiyatis akhsata: in beiden fällen ist hya von dem nachfolgenden passiven particip getrennt und das subject in die mitte genommen; nur der gebrauch des optativs ist verschieden. An unserer stelle bezeichnet er den einer aufforderung fast gleichkommenden wunsch.

Eine gewisse wahrscheinlichkeit, dass hya das pronomen hya nicht sein kann, sehe ich in dem umstand, dass mit ausnahme des einen hya amakham tauma (in gleicher wiederholung Bh. I 8 und A 12) die verbindung hya + genetiv + substantiv durchaus ungewönlich ist. (Ein solches hya (oder tya) is dagegen beliebt zwischen subst. und nachfolgenden gen. Bh. I, 85. 89. 95. II, 69. III, 38 Bh. I, 69. 71. II, 27. 35. 40. 46. 55.)

Die positiv ausgedrückte aufforderung wird mit den folgenden injunctiven nochmals in negativer form wiederholt. Die alte erklärung von ma thadaya ist nun natürlich unmöglich geworden; es ist die 2. pers sing. des injunctivs wie die folgenden formen auch. Ich ziehe th.d zur ai. wurzel çad „abfallen" und sehe dieselbe wurzel im german, hatjan „hassen", für das man meines wissens noch keine anknüpfung in den verwandten sprachen gefunden hat (s. Kluge, Etym. Wb. s. v.). Die bedeutungsentwicklung ist „abfallen, verwerfen, ver abscheuen, hassen" An unserer stelle haben wir die wahl zu übersetzen „falle nicht ab" oder „verabscheue nicht". Im letzern falle bildet ap. thad den übergang in der bedeutungsentwicklung von ai. çad zu german. hassen. Die zweite bedeutung „verabscheuen" darf auf grund des durch die medische übersetzung festgestellten sinns

C.

Gaubaruva, a Patisuvarian, spear-bearer of Darius the king.

D.

Aspacana, quiver-bearer?, a server of the arrows of Darius the king.

E.

This (is) a Macian.

---

vorgezogen werden, wärend ich andererseits die richtigkeit meiner erklärung der ganzen stelle mit der med. und assyr. übersetzung mehr in übereinstimmung finde als die frühere interpretation: Med. quae Oromazdis doctrina eam ne malam putes. Assyr. ,,was Ormuzd befiehlt, lehne dich nicht dagogen auf" (Bezold). Für ma *starava* scheint mir weder Bollensens übersetzung ,,falle nicht ab" noch Bartholomae's ähnliche ,,verliere, verlasse nicht den pfad" genügend von den vorhergehenden aufforderungen sich abzuheben, und ich halte daher Bartholomae's zweiten vorschlag ,,beflecke ihn (den pfad) nicht" (zu avest. a-staraieti) für richtiger." For Thumbs' connection between O. P. th*a*d and Skt. çad, cf. Brugmann, Grunde. I. 397.

THE INSCRIPTIONS OF XERXES AT PERSEPOLIS.

(PERSIAN, MEDIAN, ASSYRIAN.)

TRANSLATION.

D.

UPON EACH ONE OF THE FOUR PILLARS OF THE ENTRANCES TO THE PALACE OF XERXES.

A great god (is) Auramazda who created this earth, who created yonder heaven, who created man, who created the spirit? of man, who created Xerxes king, one king of many, one lord of many. I (am) Xerxes the great king, king of kings, king of the countries, possessing many kinds of people, king of this great earth far and wide, the son of Darius the king, the Achaemenide. Says Xerxes the great king by the grace of Auramazda, this entrance possessing all countries I made; much else (that is) beautiful (was) done by* this Persian (people) which I did and which my father did; whatever (that has been) done seems beautiful, all that we did by the grace of Auramazda. Says Xerxes the king let Auramazda protect me and my kingdom and what (was) done by me and what (was) done by my father, (all) this let Auramazda protect.

G.

UPON THE PILLARS ON THE WESTERN SIDE OF THE PALACE, WHERE XERXES IS REPRESENTED STANDING WITH TWO ATTENDANTS.

Xerxes the great king, king of kings, the son of Darius the king, the Achaemenide.

---

*I have followed the old interpretation. (Cf. Oppert, Journal Asiat. XIX, 177 "avec cette Perse, aidé par ce peuple Perse"). If we can regard ana as the equivalent of the Avest. prep. ana (cf. Gr. $\dot{\alpha}\nu\alpha$) we can translate "through Persia" (Parsa being the instr. sing. or better acc. plr.; Cf. Grammar, 86, B. Note 1.) Cf. Zeitschrift für vergleichende Sprachforschung. p. 127 [1891]).

Ea.

UPON THE WALL BY THE STAIRS OF THE PALACE.

A great god (is) Auramazda who created this earth, who created yonder heaven, who created man, who created the spirit? of man, who made Xerxes king, one king of many, one lord of many. I (am) Xerxes the great king, king of kings, king of the provinces possessing many kinds of people, king of this great earth far and wide, son of Darius the king, the Achaemenide. Says Xerxes the great king by the grace of Auramazda this palace (lit. seat) I made; let Auramazda protect me with the gods and my kingdom and what (was) done by me.

Eb.

The above inscription is repeated on the western stairs of the palace.

Ca.

UPON THE HIGHEST PILLAR NEAR THE SOUTHERN STAIRS.

A great god (is) Auramazda who created this earth, who created yonder heaven, who created man, who created the spirit? of man, who made Xerxes king, one king of many, one lord of many. I (am) Xerxes the great king, king of kings, king of the provinces possessing many kinds of people, king of this great earth far and wide, son of Darius the king, the Achaemenide. Says Xerxes the great king by the grace of Aura* Mazda this palace (lit. seat) Darius the king made who (was) my father; let Auramazda protect me with the gods and what (was) done by my father Darius the king, (all) this let Auramazda protect with the gods.

---

*Notice that the two members of the compound are separated. Cf. Original Text of the Inscriptions.

Cb.

The above inscription is repeated upon the walls of the southern stairs.

A.
UPON THE STAIRS OF THE PALACE.

A great god (is) Auramazda who created this earth, who created yonder heaven, who created man, who created the spirit ? of man, who made Xerxes king, one king of many, one lord of many. I (am) Xerxes the great king, king of kings, king of the provinces possessing many kinds of people, king of this great earth far and wide, the son of Darius the king, the Achaemenide. Says Xerxes the great king what (was) done by me here and what (was) done by me afar, all this I did by the grace of Auramazda; let Auramazda protect me with the gods and my kingdom and what (was) done by me.

The Inscription of Xerxes at Alvend.

(PERSIAN, MEDIAN, ASSYRIAN.)

F.

The following inscription is engraven upon two niches cut into a small rock:

TRANSLATION.

A great god (is) Auramazda, who (is) greatest of the gods, who created this earth, who created yonder heaven, who created man, who created the spirit? of man, who made Xerxes king, one king of many, one lord of many. I (am) Xerxes the great king, king of kings, king of the provinces possessing many kinds of people, king of this great earth far and wide, the son of Darius the king, the Achaemenide.

The Inscription upon the Vase of Count Caylus.

(PERSIAN, MEDIAN, ASSYRIAN, EGYPTIAN.)

Qa.

This vase contains the three customary forms of cuneiform writing and a line of Egyptian hieroglyphics. The relic is preserved in Paris. Four fragments of similar alabaster vases containing the same quadrilingual inscription have been found by W. K. Loftus in Susa, and are to be seen to-day in the British Museum.

TRANSLATION.

I (am) Xerxes, the great king.

The Inscription at Van.
K.
(PERSIAN, MEDIAN, ASSYRIAN.)

This inscription is about sixty feet from the plain below, engraven upon a niche in an enormous rock which rises to the perpendicular height of one hundred feet.

TRANSLATION.

A great god (is) Auramazda who (is) the greatest of the gods, who created this earth, who created yonder heaven, who created man, who created the spirit? of man, who made Xerxes king, one king of many, one lord of many. I (am) Xerxes the great king, king of kings, king of the provinces possessing many kinds of people, king of this great earth far and wide, the son of Darius the king, the Achaemenide. Says Xerxes the king, Darius, the king who (was) my father, he by the grace of Auramazda did what (was) beautiful to a great extent, and he commanded to carve this place ——? he did not make the inscriptions inscribed; afterwards I commanded to inscribe this inscription; (let Auramazda protect me with the gods and my kingdom and what (has been) done by me.*)

---
*Supplied from the Assyrian version.

THE INSCRIPTION OF ARTAXERXES I. (Qb)

(PERSIAN, MEDIAN, ASSYRIAN, EGYPTIAN.)

This inscription, which is quadrilingual is engraven upon a vase which is preserved in the treasury of St. Mark's at Venice.

TRANSLATION.

Artaxerxes,* the great king.

---

*The cuneiform text spells the name of the monarch on the vase ARDAKHCASHCA. This spelling must be due either to foreign pronunciation or to the ignorance of the workman. Elsewhere the cuneiform characters given the regular ARTAKHSHATRA. Cf. Original Text of the Inscriptions.

THE INSCRIPTION OF DARIUS II. (L.)

(PERSIAN, MEDIAN, ASSYRIAN.)

TRANSLATION.

ABOVE THE POSTS OF THE WINDOWS IN THE PALACE AT PERSEPOLIS.

(This) lofty stone structure (has been) made by (one belonging to) the race of Darius the king.*

---
*The Median and Assyrian translate the last of this legend "in the house of Darius the king."

THE INSCRIPTION OF ARTAXERXES MNEMON AT SUSA.

(PERSIAN, MEDIAN, ASSYRIAN.)

This inscription is upon the base of one of the columns in the ruins of what once must have been a great palace. Much of this building was used for the pavement of other edifices by the races which in after time possessed this spot.

TRANSLATION.

a.

I (am) Artaxerxes, the great king, king of kings, the son of Darius* the king.

b.

UPON THE BASE OF THE PILLARS IN THE LARGE ROW OF COLUMNS.

This palace seems to have been fashioned after the model of that of Darius at Persepolis. In connection with this edifice it is interesting to refer to Dan. viii. 2. "And it came to pass when I saw, that I was in Susa (or Shushan) in the palace," etc.

TRANSLATION.

Says Artaxerxes the great king, king of kings, king of the countries, king of the earth, the son of Darius the king; Darius (was) the son of Artaxerxes the king; Artaxerxes (was) the son of Xerxes the king: Xerxes (was) the son of Darius the king; Darius (was) the son of Hystaspes, the Achaemenide; this building Darius, my ancestor made...............
......Artaxerxes (my) grandfather......Anakata and Mithra........by the grace of Auramazda the building I made; let Auramazda, Anahata and Mithra protect me........

---

*Cf. Grammar, 24. DARaYava(H)USH (Darius) although having a stem in u is treated like nouns whose stems end in *a*. So in Prakrit there is a strong tendency for the so-called first declension to trespass upon the others, thus breaking down the barriers which were observed by the Sanskrit.

THE INSCRIPTION OF ARTAXERXES OCHUS AT PERSEPOLIS. (P.)

(PERSIAN.)

TRANSLATION.

UPON THE STEPS OF THE PALACE.

A great god (is) Auramazda who created this earth, who created yonder heaven, who created man, who created the spirit? of man, who made me, Artaxerxes, king, one king of many, one lord of many. Says Artaxerxes the great king, king of kings, king of countries, king of the earth. I (am) the son of Artaxerxes, the king; Artaxerxes (was) the son of Darius the king; Darius (was) the son of Artaxerxes the king; Artaxerxes (was) the son of Xerxes the king; Xerxes (was) the son of Darius the king; Darius was the son of Hystaspes by name; Hystaspes was the son of Arshama by name, the Achaemenide. Says Artaxerxes the king this lofty stone structure (was) made by me during my reign (lit. under me). Says Artaxerxes the king let Auramazda and the god Mithra protect me and this country and what (was) done by me.

THE INSCRIPTION OF ARSACES.
(PERSIAN.)

TRANSLATION.
UPON THE SEAL OF GROTEFEND.

R.

Arsaces by name, son of Athiyabaushana.

PERSIAN-ENGLISH
VOCABULARY.

VOCABULARY.

For the sake of convenience in comparison, the same method of transliteration is adopted for Sanskrit and Avestan words as for Old Persian.

A.

A, — prefix, *to.* Skt., a; Avest., a; Lat. a(?) 'from'. (For postpositive a, cf. Bezz. Beitr. XIII.)

Ai, — pron. root in ai*t*a, aiv*a*.

Ait*a*, — n. pr., *this, that.* Skt. et*a*t; Avest., aet*a*d; Lat., iste; Goth., thata; Eng., that.

Ain*a*, — name of the father of Naditabira.

Aiv*a*, — *one.* Skt., ek*a*; Avest., aev*a*.

Autiyar*a*, — name of a country in Armenia.

Aur*a* or A(h)ur*a*, — 1) m., *master, ruler*; 2) f., *goddess.* Skt., asur*a*; Avest., ahur*a*.

Aur*a*mazda or A(h)ur*a*mazda, — the name of the greatest deity. Aur*a*, see above; m*a*zda, compound of m*a*z, great: Skt., mah*a*t; Lat., magnus; Goth., mag; AS., magan; Eng., might; and da, give: Skt., da; Avest., da; Lat., do: or da, know.

Akhsh, — *to see.* Skt., akshi; Lat., oc-ulus. (Cf. Paul Kretschmer in Zitsch. für vergl. Sprachforsch, p. 432 [1891]).

— with pati, *to oversee, rule.*

Akhshata, — *whole, entire, perfect.* Fem. of an adjective, akhsh*a*ta. Skt., akshata.

Agata, — nomen agentis; *comer, friend*(?). Cf. gam.

Aj(?), — *drive, do.* Skt., aj; Lat., ago. (It is possible to refer ajata to jan, smite.)

Atiy, — verbal prefix, *beyond, across.* Skt.. ati; Lat., et; Old German, anti(?); Germ., und(?); Eng., and(?).

Atha(n)gaina, — *stony, built of stone.*

Athura, — *Assyria.*

Atrina, — proper name.

Atriyadiya, — name of a month.

Ada, — *then, thereupon.*

Adakaiy, — *then.*

Adam, — *I.* Skt., aham; Avest., azem; Lat., ego; Goth., ik; AS., ik or I; Eng., I. (For kh in amakham, cf. idg. Forschungen, p. 186 [1892]; for position of maiy and mam, cf. Wachernagel, über ein Gesetz der idg. Wortstell, ibid.).

Adukanish. — name of a month.

Anahata, — Genius of the waters.

Anamaka. — name of a month.

Aniya, — 1) indef. pron., *another*; 2) *enemy?* Skt., anya; Avest., anya.

Anuv, — prep. with loc., *along, by.* Skt., anu.

Anushiya, — *follower.* See anuv and shiyu; cf. Lat., comes (con-eo).

A(n)tar, — prep. with acc., *within, in.* Skt., antar; Avest., antare; Lat., inter; Goth., undar.

Apa, — verbal prefix, *from.* Skt., apa; Avest., apa; Lat., ab; Goth., af; Eng., of.

Apatara, — *remote, another.* Comparative of apa.

Ap*a*dana, — *work, temple, building.*
Ap*a*nyaka, — *ancestor.*
Ap*a*ram, — adv., *afterward.*
Ap*a*riy, — *near by.*
Api, — *water.* Skt., ap; Avest., ap.
Apiy, — *to, also.* Skt., api; Avest., api.
Ab*a*carish, — *commerce.*
Ab*a*shta, — *law.*
Abiy, — prep. with acc., *to, against.* Skt., abhi; Avest., aibiy; Lat., ob(?), ambi.
Abish, — prep. with loc., *by, at.*
Amutha, — *there, then.* Skt., amutr*a*.
Ayadana, — acc. pl., ayadana, *sanctuaries, homes.*
Ayasta, — adv. or prep. with acc., *according to, with, unto* (?).
Ar*a*kadrish, — name of a Persian mountain.
Ar*a*kha, — name of an Armenian.
Ar*a*baya, — 1) *Arabian*; 2) *Arab, Arabia.*
Arika, — *enemy.* Skt., ari.
Ariya, — 1) *Aryan*; 2) *noble.* Skt., arya; Avest., airya; New Persian, Iran; Keltic, erin; Eng., Ir-ish.
Ariyar*a*mna or Ariyaramn*a*, — name of the great-grandfather of Darius. Ariya and r*a*m, to rejoice. (For change of stem, cf. Bartholomae, idg. Forsch., p. 180 [1892]).
Aruv*a*stam (?)
Art*a*khshatra, — *Artaxerxes.* Arta (Avest., areta), lifted up; and khsh*a*tra, kingdom.

Artavardiya, — name of one of the commanders of Darius Hystaspes.

Ardakhcashcha, — name of Artaxerxes as pronounced by the Egyptians.

Ardastana, — *high structure.*

Ardumanish, — name of one of the Persians who swore with Darius against Smerdis.

Arbira, — *Arbela*; a city upon the confines of Media.

Armaniya, — 1) *Armenian*; 2) *Armenia.*

Armina, — name of Armenia.

Arminiya, — *Armenian.*

Arshaka, — *Arsaces.*

Arshada, — name of a fortress in Arachasia.

Arshama, — name of the grandfather of Darius Hystaspes.

Arshtish, — *spear.* Skt., ṛshti; Avest., arsti.

Arshtibara, — *spear-bearer.*

Ava, — dem. pron., *this, that.* Avest., ava; Slav., ova.

Ava, — verbal prefix, *from.* Skt., ava.

Ava, — *so long.* Correl. to yava.

Avatha, — *thus.*

Avada, — 1) *there*; 2) *thither.*

— In ablative sense with suffix sa, *from that place, thence.*

Avapara, — *thence.*

Avashciy, — *whatever, anything, all.* Ava-ciy.

Avah. — *aid, guard.* Avest., avo.

Avah,— denom. from preceding.

— with prefix *patiy, to seek aid.*

Avahyaradiy,— *for this reason, therefore.* Composed of gen. of pron. ava, and loc. of rad.

Avahanam,— *village*; from root vah, to dwell. Skt., vas; Lat., vesta; Germ., woh-nen; AS., wesan; Eng., was.

Asagarta,— *Sagartian.*

Asagartiya,— *Sagartian.*

Asabari, or asbari,— *soldier*; properly, *a horseman.*

Aspacana,— a proper name in Persia. Probably from aspa, horse; according to Herodotus, the name of a man. (For aspa, cf. Meyer in idg. Forsch., p. 329 [1892]).

Asman,— *heaven.* Skt., açman.

Ashnaiy,— *near.*

Azda,— *knowledge.*

Ah,— *to be.* Skt., as; Avest., ah; Lat., es-t; Goth., is-t; Eng., is.

Ahifrastad,— *severe punishment.*

I

I,— *to go.* Skt., I; Avest., I; Lat., i-re.

— with prefix atiy, *to go beyond, carry farther.*

— with nij, *to go forth.*

— with patiy, *to go against.*

— with para, *to proceed.*

— with apari, *to follow, obey.*

Ida,— *here.* Skt., iha; Avest., idha.

Im*a*,—pron., *this*. Skt., ima; Avest., im*a*.

Im*a*ni,—name of a man in Susa, who excited a tumult against Darius.

Ish,—*to send*. Skt., ish; Avest., ish.

— with prefix fr*a*, *to send forth*.

Ishu,—*arrow*. Skt., ishu.

Izav*a*,—*tongue*.

U

(H)u,—*good, well*. It occurs only in the beginning of a compound. Skt., su; Avest., hu.

Ut*a*,—*and*. Skt., ut*a*; Avest., ut*a*.

Utan*a*,— name of one of the six who dethroned false Smerdis.

Ud,—verbal prefix. Skt., ud.

Up*a*,—prefix, *under, to*. Skt., up*a*; Avest., up*a*; Lat., sub.

Upa,—prep. with acc., *under*. Cf. above.

Up*a*d*a*r*a*(n)m*a*,—name of a man in Susiana.

Up*a*riy,—prep. with acc., *above, over*. Skt., up*a*ri; Avest., up*a*ra; Lat., super; Goth., ufar; Eng., over.

Up*a*st*a*,—*aid, help*. Upa and sta; cf. Germ., beistand.

(H)ufr*a*st*a*,—see p*a*rs.

(H)ufr*a*tu,—*Euphrates*. From u, well; and fra (perhaps a Semitic root), to flow.

(H)ub*a*rt*a*,—see b*a*r.

(H)um*a*rtiy*a*,—*possessing good men*.

(H)uv*a*khsh*a*t*a*r*a*,—name of a king of Media.

(H)uv*aj*a, — *Susiana.*

(H)uv*a*jiy*a*, — an inhabitant of Susiana.

(H)uv*a*spa, — *possessing good horses.*

(H)uv*a*ipashiy*a*, — *one's own pleasure, independence.* (h)uv*a*, self; Skt., sv*a*; Lat., suus.

Uv*a*d*a*id*a*y*a*, — name of a city in Persia.

(H)uv*a*m*a*rshiyush, — *committing suicide.* (h)uv*a*, self; Skt., sv*a*: and m*a*rsh; Avest., m*e*resh, to die.

(H)uv*a*r*a*z*a*mi or (H)uv*a*r*a*z*a*miy*a*, — *Chorasmia.*

Us, — cf. ud.

Us*a*t*a*sh*a*n*a*, — *lofty building, temple.* Us (see above) and t*a*sh; Skt., t*a*ksh; Avest., t*a*sh, to form; Lat., tig-mum.

(H)ushk*a*, — *dry.* Avest., hushk*a*. (Cf. idg. Forschungen, Bartholomae, p. 488 [1892]).

Uz*a*ma, — *cross.*

Uhy*a*ma, — name of a castle in Armenia.

K

K*a*, — interrog. pron., *who.* Skt., k*a*; Avest., k*a*; Lat., qui.

— with personal or relative pronoun having an indefinite force: *(who)ever.*

K*a*uf*a*, — *mountain.*

K*a*t*a*p*a*tuk*a*, — *Cappadocia.*

K*a*n, — *to dig, scratch.* Skt., kh*a*n; Avest., k*a*n; Lat., cun-iculus.

— with prefix av*a*, *to throw down with violence, displace.*

— with ni, *to dig down, destroy.*

— with vi, *to destroy.*

Kamana, — *desirous, faithful.* Skt., kam, to desire; few?

Ka(m)pada, — name of a province in Media.

Ka(m)bujiya, — *Cambyses.*

Kar, — *to do.* Skt., kṛ; Avest.. kar; Lat., cre-o.
— with prefix pari, *to guard.*

Kashciy, — indef. pron., *whoever.*
— with preceding naiy, *no one.*

Karka, — name of a people.

Kapishakani, — name of a fortress in Arachasia.

Kama, — *wish, desire.* Skt., kama.

Kara, — 1) *people*; 2) *army.* Cf. kar.

Kuganaka, — name of a city in Persia.

Kud(u)ru, — name of a city in eastern Media.

Kuru, — *Cyrus.*

Kushiya, — name of a people.

Kh

Khshatra — nom. and acc., khshatram; *rule, kingdom.* Skt., kshatra; Avest., khshathra.

Khshatrapavan, — nom., khshatrapava; *satrap.* From khshatra (cf. above) and pa (to guard, protect).

Khshathrita, — name of a man who excited a tumult against Darius in Media.

Khshapar, — acc., khshapa; *night.* Skt., kshap; Avest., khshap.

Khshayathiya, — *king.* (Cf. Brugmann in Idg. Forschungen, p. 177 [1892]).

Khshayarsha, — *Xerxes.*

Khshi (?)
— with prefix pati, *to rule, reign*. (It is possible to refer patiyakhshaiy to akhsh, see).

Khshnas, — *to know*. (Perhaps connected with Skt., Jna; Avest., khshna; Lat., co-gno-sco; Goth., kaun; Germ., kann; Eng., know, can).

G

Gaitha, — *flock, herd*.

Gaubaruva, — *Gobryas*. The name of a man.

Gaumata, — name of a Magian.

Gausha, — acc. dual, gausha; *ear*. Avest., gaosha.

Ga(n)dutava, — name of a country in western Arachosia.

Ga(n)dara, — name of a country near the Indus.

Gam, — *to go*. Skt., gam; Avest., gam; Lat., venio (for guemio?); Goth., quam; Germ., kommen; Eng., come.

— with prefix a, *to approach, come*.

— with ham, *to gather one's self together*.

— with para, *to depart*.

Garb, — *to seize, take*. Skt., grabh; Avest., garep; Germ., greif-en (?); Eng., gripe (?).

Garmapada, — name of a month.

Gasta, — *revealed, declared*. Skt., gad.

Gathu, — 1) *foundation, firm place*; 2) *throne*. Avest., gathu.

Gud, — Skt., guh; Avest., guz.

— with prefix apa, *to conceal*.

Gub, — *to speak*; middle, *to be called* or *named*.

C

Caishpi, — son of Achaemenes.
Cashma, — *eye.*
Ca, — encl., *and.* Skt., ca; Avest., ca; Lat., que.
Ciy, — neut., ciy and cish; *who, what.* Skt., cit; Avest., ci.
— cishciy, *whatever.* (For change of etym. t to sh before c, cf. idg. Forschungen, p. 488 [1891]).
— anivashciy, *some other.*
Ciya(n)karam, — *how many, manifold.*
Cicikhri, — name of a man.
Cita, — *so long as.*
Citra, — *seed, offspring.*
Citra(n)takhma, — name of a man.

J

Jad, — *to supplicate, pray; to grant prayer.*
Jatar, — nom. jata, *enemy.* Cf. jan.
Jan, — *to smite.* Skt., han; Avest., jan.
— with prefix ava, *to smite down, kill.*
— with fra, *to cut off.*
Jiv, — *to live.* Skt., jiv; Avest., jiv; Lat., vivo.
Jiva, — *life.*

T

Taiyiya or maiyiya, — doubtful word (*witness ?*).
Tauma, — *race, family.* Avest., taokhma.
Takabara, — epithet of the Greeks, *wearing crowns, wearing long hair.*

T*a*khm*a*spad*a*,— name of one of the commanders of Darius.

T*a*khs,— *to construct, build.* Skt., t*a*ksh; Avest., t*a*sh.

— with prefix h*a*m, *to work together, help, work.*

T*a*c*a*r*a*,— *building, temple.*

T*a*r,— *to cross, put across.* Skt., tr; Avest., t*a*r; Lat., in-tra-re, trans; Old German, durh; Eng., through.

— with prefix fr*a*, *to go forward.*

— with vi, *to put over* or *across.*

T*a*r*a*d*a*r*a*y*a*,— *across the sea*; from t*a*r*a*, across, and d*a*r*a*y*a*, the sea.

T*a*rs,— *to tremble, fear.* Skt., tr*a*s; Avest., t*a*rs-ti.

T*a*r*a*v*a*,— name of a city in Yutia of Persia.

Tigr*a*,— name of a fortress in Armenia.

Tigr*a*,— *Tigris*; perhaps feminine of an adjective, tigr*a*, sharp. Skt., tij. Cf. Dionys. perig. v. 984, "The Medes call the Tigris an arrow."

Tigr*a*kh*a*ud*a*,— name of a Scythian tribe.

Tuv*a*m,— *thou.* Skt., tv*a*m; Avest., thw*a*m; Lat., tu; Germ., du. (Cf. Wachernagel, über ein Gesetz der idg. Wortstellung, idg. Forsch., p. 403 [1892]).

Ty*a*,— rel. pron., *who, that.* Skt., y*a*; Avest., hy*a*;

— ty*a*patiy, *whatever.*

Th

Thaigarci, — name of a month.

Thakata, — *then* (?). (This meaning is a conventional one. A recent theory proposes a widely different signification, but at present both the etymology and interpretation of the word are doubtful).

Thatagush, — name of a people.

Thad, — *to go, err* (?). (Perhaps connected with: Skt., sad; Lat., sideo; Got., sat; Eng., sit).

Thah, — *to say, speak.* Thatiy for Thahatiy.

Thukhra, — name of a Persian.

Thuravahara, — name of a month.

Thard, — *kind, sort, manner.*

Tr

Trar.

— with prefix ni, *to restore.*

Tritiya, — *third.* Skt., tritiya; Avest., thritya; Lat., tertius; Goth., thridya; Eng., third.

D

Daushtar, — *friend.*

Dan, — *to flow.*

Dar, — *to hold, to hold one's self; to delay, halt.* Skt., dhṛ; Avest., dar.

Daraya, — *sea.*

Darsh, — *to dare, subdue.* Skt., dhṛsh; Avest., daresh; Eng., durst.

Darsham, — *strongly, very.*

Darshama, — *insolence, ferocity, violence.*

Dasta,— *hand.* Skt., hasta; Avest., zasta.

Dashabari,— *stretching out the hand, submissive.*

Dahyaush,— *region, province.* Skt., dasyu; Avest., daqyu.

Da,— *to give.* Skt., da; Avest., da; Lat., da-re.

Da,— *to place, create, do, make.* Skt., dha; Lat., con-do, cre-do; AS., dom; Eng., doom.

Da,— *to know, understand.* Avest., da.

Data,— *law.* Cf. da.

Dadarshi,— a name of an Armenian and Persian.

Daduhya,— one of the six who, with Darius Hystaspes, deprived false Smerdis of his kingdom.

Darayava(h)u,— *Darius.* Cf. dar; for second member of the compound, cf. Skt. vasu, good; as a noun, wealth: perhaps from vas, to shine (like Eng. splendid). Cf. Lat., us-tus, Ves-uvius; Eng., East.

Dasyaman,— *he who stretches forth, serves; an attendant* (perhaps).

Di,— pron. root, *this.* (Cf. Wachernagel, über ein Gesetz der idg. Wortstellung, idg. Forsch., p. 405 [1892]).

Di,— *to see.* Avest., di.

Di,— *to remove, take away.*

Dida,— *castle.*

Dipi,— *letter, inscription.* Perhaps connected with Skt., lip.

Dubana,— name of a country in Babylonia.

Dura,— loc. duraiy, duray, and durai; *far, distant.* Skt., dura.

Duruj, — *to deceive, be false.* Skt., druh; Avest., druj.
Duruva, — *firm, well, sound, secure.* Skt., dhruva.
Duvaishtam, — *a long time.*
Duvar, — *to make, accomplish* (?).
Duvara, — *door, court.* Skt., dvara; Avest., dvara.
Duvarthi, — *gate.*
Duvitatarnam, — *separately* (?), *for a long time* (?).
Duvitiya, — *second.* Skt., dvitiya; Avest., bitya; Lat., duo, bis; Goth., tvai; AS., twa; Eng., two.
Dushiyara, — *misfortune*; from dush. Skt., dus, ill, and yara; Avest., yare.
Drauga, — *lie, falsehood.* Cf. duruj.
Draujana, — *false, deceiving.*
Dra(n)ga, — *a long time.*

N

Naiba, — *beautiful, pretty.*
Naiy, — *not.*
Naditabira, — name of a man who excited opposition against Darius in Babylon.
Napa, — *grandson.* Skt., napat; Avest., napat; Lat., nepo(t)s; AS., nefa.
Nabukudracara, — name of a Babylonian king.
Nabunita, — name of the last Babylonian king.
Navama, — *ninth.* Skt., navama; Avest., navan; Lat., novem; Goth., niun; AS., nigan; Eng., nine.

Nam*a*n,— *name.* Skt., nam*a*n; Avest., nam*ą*n; Lat., nomen; Goth., namo; Eng., name.

Nau,— *ship.* Skt., naus; Lat., navis.

Nah*a*,— *nose.* Skt., nasa.

Ni,— *to conduct, lead.* Skt., ni.

Nij,— verbal prefix, *from.* Skt., nis; Avest., nish.

Nip*a*d.— loc. nip*a*diy, *footprint, on foot.* Ni, down (Skt., ni; Lat., in; AS., in), and p*a*d, foot (Skt., p*a*d; Avest., padh*a*; Lat., pe(d)s; Goth., fotus; Eng., foot).

Nisay*a*,— name of a country in Media.

Ny*a*ka,— *grandfather.* Avest., nyaka.

Nuram,— *now.*

P

P*a*ishiyauvada,— name of a region.

P*a*t,— *to fall.* Skt., p*a*t; Lat., peto.

— with prefix ud, *to rise up.*

P*a*tiy,— prep. and verbal prefix. 1) *in*; 2) *against*; 3) *throughout.* Often postpositive. Skt., prati; Avest., paiti.

P*a*tik*a*ra,— *image, effigy.*

P*a*tigr*a*bana,— name of a city in Parthia.

P*a*tip*a*dam,— *in its own place.* From p*a*tiy (cf. above) and p*a*d (cf. nip*a*d).

P*a*tish,— with acc., *towards.* Cf. p*a*tiy.

P*a*thi,— *way, road.* Skt., p*a*th*a*; Avest., panth*a*n; Lat., pon(t)s; Old Germ., pad, fad; AS., padh; Eng., path.

P*a*rauva,— *eastern.*

Paraga, — name of a Persian mountain.

Parana, — *former.*

Para, — prep., postpositive, and verbal prefix, *from, backward.* Skt., para; Lat., per; Goth., fra; Old Germ., fer; Germ., ver; AS., for, as in Eng., forgive.

Pariy, — prep. and verbal prefix, *around, about, concerning.* Skt., pari; Avest., pairi.

Paru, — gen. plur., parunam and paruvnam; *much, many.* Skt., puru; Avest., pouru; Lat., plus; Goth., filu; Germ., viel.

Paruva, — *anterior eastern;* acc. neut., paruvam: *before.* Avest., paourva.

Paruviya, — *before, anterior;* in abl. sense, haca paruviyata. Skt. Ved., purvya; Avest., paourvya.

Paruzana, — gen. plur., paruzananam and paruvzananam; *possessing many kinds of peoples.*

Parthava, — *Parthia.*

Pars, — 1) *to ask;* 2) *to inquire about something.* Skt., prach; Avest., pares; Lat., preco; Goth., frah; Germ., fragen.

— with preceding (h)u, *to examine carefully, punish;* part. (h)u-frastam.

— with prefix pati, *to examine, read.*

Pasa, — *after.*

Pasava, — *afterwards, thereafter.* Pasa and ava.

Pa, — *to protect, sustain.* Skt., pa; Avest., pa; Lat., pa-vi, pa-scor.

Patishuvari, — a race inhabiting a portion of Persia.

Parsa, — *Persia, Persian.*

Pitar,—*father.* Skt., pitr; Avest., pita; Lat., pater; Goth., fadar; Germ., vater; AS., faeder; Eng., father. Cf. pa.

Pish,—*to scrape, graze.* Skt., pish; Lat., pinso.

— with prefix ni, *to write on.*

Pirava.—*Nile.*

Putiya,—name of a people.

Putra,—*son.* Skt., putra; Avest., puthra; Lat., puer (?).

F

Fra,—verbal prefix. *before, for.* Skt., pra; Avest., fra; Lat., pro; Eng., fore.

Fratama,—*first, leader.*

Framana,—*authority, command, precepts.*

Fravarti,—proper name, *Phraortes.*

Fraharvam,—acc. neut. in adverbial sense, *altogether.* From fra and harva, haruva.

Frada,—name of a ruler in Margia.

B

Baga,—*god.* Skt., bhaga; Avest., bagha; Goth., ga-bigs.

Bagabukhsha,—name of one of those who with Darius dethroned false Smerdis; *Megabyzos.*

Bagabigna,—name of a Persian.

Ba(n)d,—*to bind,* Skt., bandh; Avest., band; Goth., bindan; Eng., bind.

Ba(n)daka,—*subject, servant.*

Bar,— *to bear, sustain, protect.* Skt., bhṛ; Avest., bar; Lat., fero; Goth., bairan; AS., beran; Eng., bear.

— with prefix pati, *to bring back, replace, restore.*

— with para, *to bear away.*

— with fra, *to carry off, assign.*

Bardiya,— name of the brother of Cambyses, *Smerdis.*

Bakhtri,— *Bactria.*

Bagayadi,— name of a month.

Baji,— *tribute*; from root baj.   Skt., bhaj, to allot.

Babiru,— *Babylon.*

Babiruviya,— *Babylonian.*

Bu,— *to be.* Skt., bhu; Avest., bu; Lat., fuo, fui, perhaps bam (in amabam); AS., beom; Germ., bin; Eng., be.

Bumi,— *ground, earth.* Skt., bhumi; Avest., bumi.

Bratar,— *brother.* Skt., bhratṛ; Avest., bratar; Lat., frater; Goth., brothar; AS., brodher; Eng., brother.

M

Maka,— name of a people.

Magu,— *Magian*, a Median people from whom the priests were elected.

Maciya,— name of a people.

Mathishta,— *the greatest, leader.*

Man,— *to think, ponder.* Skt., man; Avest., man; Lat., mens; Germ., meinen.

Man,— *to remain.* Avest., man; Lat., maneo.

M*a*r,— *to die.* Skt., mr̥; Avest., m*a*r; Lat., morior; AS., mordh.

M*a*rgu,— name of a region east and north of Areia.

M*a*rtiya,— 1) *mortal, man*; cf. m*a*r above. 2) name of a man who excited a tumult against Darius. In P. the gen. sing. is contracted to m*a*rtihy*a*.

M*a*rduniy*a*,— name of a man, *Mardonius.*

M*a*,— *to measure.* Skt., ma; Avest., ma; Lat., meto.

— with prefix **a**, past part., am*a*ta, *tested, tried, prolonged.*

M*a*,— prohibitive particle, *not.* Skt., ma; Avest., ma.

M*a*ty*a*,— *that not, lest.*

M*a*d*a*,— *Median, Media.*

M*a*niy*a*,— *place of remaining, dwelling.* Cf. man.

M*a*rg*a*y*a* or M*a*rg*a*v*a*,— *Margianian.*

M*a*h*a*,— *month*; contracted gen. m*a*hy*a*. Skt., mas*a*; Lat., mensis; AS., mona; Eng., month.

M(i)thr*a*,— name of a Persian God.

Mudr*a*y*a*,— *Egypt*; nom. plur., *Egyptians.*

Y

Y*a*una,— *Ionian, Ionia.* Skt., Y*a*v*a*n*a*.

Y*a*th*a*,— 1) *as, when*; 2) *because*; 3) *in order that, that.* From rel. root, y*a*.

Y*a*d*a*,— *duty.*

Y*a*diy,— 1) *if*; 2) *when.* Skt., y*a*di; Avest., yedhi.

— with p*a*diy, *if perchance.*

Y*a*n*a*iy,— (?)

Yata,—1) *during, while*; 2) *until.* From rel. root, ya.
Yana,—*favor.* Avest., yana.
Yava,—*as long as.* Skt., yavat.
Yutiya,—name of a region in Persia.
Yuviya,—*canal.*

R

Rauca,—acc. sing., rauca; *day.* Connected with Skt., ruc, to shine; Lat., lucco; AS., leoht; Eng., light.
Rauta,—*river.*
Rakha,—name of a city in Persia.
Raga,—name of a district in Media.
Rad (?),—Skt., rah.
— with prefix ava, *to relinquish, leave.*
Ras,—*to come.* Desiderative: cf. Brugmann in idg. Forsch., p. 173 (1892).
— with prefix para, *to arrive.*
— with prefix ni, *to descend.*
Rad,—*joy, delight.*
— loc. sing., radiy with gen., *for the sake of.*
— avahyaradiy, *for the sake of this thing, for this reason.*
Rasta,—*right.*

V

Vain,—*to see, behold.* The middle is used in the passive sense. Avest., vaen.
Vaumisa,—name of a Persian.

Vaj, — *to lead.* Skt., vah; Avest., vaz; AS., wegan.

Vayaspara, — name of a Persian.

Var, — *to declare, make (one) believe, convince.*

Varkana, — *Hyrcania.*

Vardana, — nom. sing., vardanam, *fortified town, city, state.* Connected with Skt. vr̥dh, to increase; Avest., va-red; AS., waldan, weald.

Vasiy, — *much, very, greatly.* (Possibly connected with Greek ἑκών, "nach Wunsch". Bartholomae).

Vashna, — *desire, power, grace.* Cf. vas, to desire.

Vazraka, — *great.*

Vahyazdata, — name of a man who excited a tumult against Darius Hystaspes.

Vahauka, — name of a Persian.

Va, — enclitic particle, *or.* Skt., va; Lat., ve.

Vith, — 1) *clan*; 2) *race, fellow.*

Vithiya, — *pertaining to the same race.*

Vithin (?), — *possessing the same race.* The instr. plur. vithibish, which alone justifies the supposition of the existence of this adjective, I have explained in grammar (86, c) as from noun vith.

Vida, — (?)

Vidarna, — name of a Persian.

Vi(n)dafra, — name of a Mede.

Vi(n)dafrana, — name of a Persian.

Viyakhna, — name of a month.

Viyatarayam, — see tar.

Vivana, — name of a Persian.

Vis*a*,—*all, every.* Skt., viçva.

Vis*a*dahyu,—acc. sing. masc. visadahyum, *possessing all provinces.*

Visp*a*z*a*n*a*,—gen. plur. masc. vispazanam, *possessing all kinds of peoples.*

Vishtasp*a*,—*Hystaspes*, the father of Darius.

S

S*a*ka,—*Scythian, Scythia.*

S*a*ku(n)k*a*,—name of a man who excited opposition among the Sakae against Darius Hystaspes.

S*a*n,—(?)

— with prefix vi, *to destroy.*

S*a*r,—*to kill.*(?)

Sik*a*y*a*uv*a*ti,—name of a fortress in Media.

Sugud*a*,—*Sogdiana.*

Skudr*a*,—name of a people.

St*a*r,—*to sin.*(?)

St*a*,—*to stand.* Skt., stha; Avest., sta; Lat., sta-re; AS., standan; Eng., stand.

— with prefix av*a* (caus.), *to establish, constitute.*

— with ni (caus.), *to enjoin, command.*

Stan*a*,—*place.*

Sp*a*rd*a*,—name of a people.

Sh

Sh*a* and Shi,—stem of a pron. encl., 3 pers. Skt., s*a*; Avest., he. (Cf. Wackernagel, über ein Gesetz der idg. Wortstellung, idg. Forsch., p. 404 [1892]).

Sharastibara, — *bow-bearer*; or perhaps for arshtibara, *spear-bearer*.

Shiyati, — *spirit, intelligence, wisdom.* (?) (shayatim, P.)

Shiyu, — *to go, set out.*

Shuguda, — see Suguda.

Z

Zara(n)ka, — *Drangiana.*

Zazana, — name of a fortified town near Babylon.

Zura, — *power.*

Zurakara, — *despot.* From zura (see above) and kara (see kar).

H

Haina. — *army.* Skt., sena; Avest., haena.

Hauv, — *this.* Skt., a-sau; Avest. hau.

Hakhamani, — *Achaemenes*, originator of the race of the Achaemenides.

Hakhamanishiya, — *of the race of Achaemenides.*

Hangmatana, — *Ecbatana*; leading city of Media, at the foot of the mountains of Alvend. From ham (together), and gam (to go).

Haca, — prep. with ablative, *from.* Avest., haca.

Ha(n)j, — *to draw, throw.*

— with fra, *to throw forth.*

Had, — *to sit.* Skt., sad; Avest., had; Lat., sedeo; AS., sittan; Eng., sit.

— witn prefix ni (caus.), *to constitute, establish.*

Hada,— prep. with instrumental, *with*. Skt., saha; Avest., hadha.

Hadish,— *place, dwelling, royal seat, palace.* Cf. had.

Ha(n)duga,— *edict.*

Handita,— name of a Babylonian.

Ham,— verbal prefix, *together with*. Skt., sam Avest., ham.

Hama,— *together, all.* Skt., sama; Avest., hama: Lat., simul; Goth., sama; Germ., zusammen: AS., same.

Hamapitar,— *having a common father.* From hama and pitar.

Hamara,— *war.* Skt., samara.

Hamarana,— nom. and acc. sing., hamaranam; *conflict, battle.*

Hamatar,— *having a common mother.* From ham and matar. Skt., matr; Lat., mater; Eng., mother. Cf. ma.

Hamitriya,— *rebellious.*

Haraiva,— name of a country, *Area.*

Harauvati,— loc. Harauvataiya, *Arachosia.*

Haruva,— *all, every.* Skt., sarva; Avest., haruva; Lat., salvus.

Hashitiya,— *rebellious.*

Hashiya,— neut. hashiyam, *true.*

Hin(d)u,— *India*; region near the river Indus. Skt., sindhu; Avest., hindu.

Humavarka,—appellation of the race of the Scythians.

Hyapara,— acc. in adverbial sense; also with patiy, *again*. From hya and apara.

www.ingramcontent.com/pod-product-compliance
Lightning Source LLC
Chambersburg PA
CBHW020843160426
43192CB00007B/760